CALLING ALL RADICALS

Jan 2012

Jim ~

For my partner
in crime.
with much respect
& Until la victoria!

Sarah

ALSO BY GABRIEL THOMPSON

There's No José Here (Nation Books)

CALLING ALL RADICALS

HOW GRASSROOTS ORGANIZERS
CAN SAVE OUR DEMOCRACY

Gabriel Thompson

Nation Books
New York
www.nationbooks.org

CALLING ALL RADICALS:
How Grassroots Organizers Can Save Our Democracy

Published by
Nation Books
A Member of the Perseus Books Group
116 East 16th Street, 8th Floor
New York, NY 10003

Nation Books is a copublishing venture of the Nation Institute
and the Perseus Books Group.

Nation Books titles are available at special discounts for bulk purchases
in the United States by corporations, institutions, and other organizations. For more information, please contact the Special Markets
Department at Perseus Books Group, 2300 Chestnut Street, Suite 200,
Philadelphia, PA 19103, or call (800) 255-1514, or
e-mail special.markets@perseusbooks.com

Library of Congress Cataloging-in-Publication Data is available.

ISBN-10: 1-56858-367-2
ISBN-13: 978-1-56858-367-9

9 8 7 6 5 4 3 2 1

Book design by Astrid deRidder

Printed in the United States of America

Washing one's hands of the conflict between the powerful and the powerless means to side with the powerful, not to be neutral.

—Paulo Freire

CONTENTS

Introduction

COMMUNITY ORGANIZERS AS DEMOCRACY BUILDERS
Sparking a Revival by Going Beyond the Vote

> *People who want to understand democracy*
> *should spend less time in the library with Aristotle*
> *and more time on the buses and in the subway.*
> —Simeon Strunsky[1]

It had the feel of a mandatory meeting. I had received a call two weeks ago from an organization called Black Veterans for Social Justice, who wanted me to do a workshop for them on tenant rights. Though I was excited—their name alone is great—I was also apprehensive about going into an all-black organization and talking to people about their rights as if I was some sort of white prophet. For six months I'd been working at my first real job after college—as an organizer at the Pratt Area Community Council (PACC), a nonprofit organization active in central Brooklyn. Now, looking out at the crowd that had gathered in front of me, I saw a room full of people bouncing their legs and staring at the ceiling. While scrawling a last minute note to myself, I took another quick glimpse around the room and realized the entire group was made up of women. Thirty agitated African-American women, forced to sit through some boring lecture by a young white guy. This had the potential for disaster.

I started with a question.

"Is Black Veterans an all-female organization?" I asked the group. I knew it wasn't. A lady in the front row looked at me—hard. "No, but we're all women here. Is that a problem?"

"No, of course not," I said hurriedly, feeling blood rush to my face and wondering if I had just made a mistake. "I was only thinking about tenants and tenant history, and other social movements. I mean, take the civil rights movement—who do you think of when you think of the civil rights movement?"

Someone in the back shouted Martin Luther King Jr., another mentioned Malcolm X. "Okay, let's take King," I said. "Does anyone here remember what started the civil rights movement, what made King famous for the first time?"

A long silence. "Yeah, it was the big bus boycott," the same woman in the front finally said. "The Montgomery Bus Boycott."

"Yeah, I think that's right," I replied, grateful for her response. "Most historians say that the Montgomery Bus Boycott started the civil rights movement, and it was the first time that many Americans had heard of King. But does anyone know who called the boycott, who started the whole thing?" I could tell by their blank stares that most had never contemplated the question.

"It was King," a woman in the back finally answered after a long silence. "He didn't think Rosa Parks should have to get up for a white man." She dragged out these last three words, making sure I understood.

"No, he definitely didn't," I answered. "But he actually didn't call the boycott. It was a group called the Women's Political Council, the WPC, that made the boycott happen. It was the Women's Political Council that decided that blacks in Montgomery needed to boycott the buses. And they called the boycott, printed out the flyers, organized the whole thing. Once they'd done that, many of the men were still afraid to publicly support the boycott, but by that time they didn't have much choice." From the looks on their faces I could tell that the women liked this idea. A few who had had their elbows resting on their knees peered up, curious.

I continued, feeling more confident. "I don't have to tell you all about what women have done; you know yourself. So I think it's appropriate that only women are here right now, because it is the women who have made up the greatest social movements in this country. It was women who started and sustained the tenant movement. And you know this, too: it's the men who get the credit."

"That's right," someone chimed in. "You know what they say: behind every man is a strong woman."

Voices rose in unison to second this notion, and I found that the women were now interested, ready to engage in discussion. In five minutes history had allowed a connection between very different people, had reframed the whole context of our meeting, had connected us at the hip with giants. Suddenly the women could imagine themselves in relation to the Women's Political Council—as people whose actions might have a serious impact. Here we were, in a stuffy, poorly lit room in some anonymous basement in Brooklyn, sitting on cheap folding chairs laid out in somebody's haphazard design. How many social movements had begun this way?

FINDING A VOICE

Though it was only a phone call, Lourdes still hadn't made it. Her one-year-old daughter, Stephanie, had recently been diagnosed with lead poisoning. A friend at her church had referred her to our organization for assistance. When we went over to her apartment to test the paint, we discovered lead levels more than a hundred times over the safety threshold. The deteriorating paint in Lourdes's home was causing permanent brain damage to her daughter.

After we got the results, I explained to Lourdes that she ought to call the city immediately and register a complaint regarding the lead. She assured me that she would make the call as soon as she hung up. Two days later, I asked her if the building inspectors had come out yet.

"I didn't call, but I will," she told me. "I had to do something else, but I'll call right now, I promise."

I called her back the next day to check in. To my bewilderment, she still hadn't called. And then I realized what was probably going on.

"Lourdes, you know that it doesn't matter if you don't have any papers, right?" I asked. "We work with many undocumented families, and you have the same rights to safe housing as anyone else. The city won't ask you any questions about that. They'll just check for lead. If you want, we can make the call together from the office."

The next day Lourdes did come into the office, and we made the call. Inspectors came out and found numerous violations. When the landlord refused to correct the problem, the city did the repairs themselves. Seeing that progress was actually possible and that her immigration status hadn't caused a problem helped alleviate some of Lourdes's initial feelings of fear.

Two months later, we were sitting in the backyard of our office, discussing logistics for a large community meeting we were planning with the commissioner of health to demand action on the lead poisoning epidemic plaguing central Brooklyn. After the successful effort to get her apartment fixed, Lourdes had joined our organization and was one of fifteen parents gathered in a circle. Toward the end of the meeting, we divided up the roles that would need to be filled at the upcoming event, from welcoming people and collecting donations to providing child care and testifying in front of the commissioner. Lourdes, as usual, stayed quiet throughout. When we broke up the meeting, however, she tapped me on the shoulder and pulled me aside.

"Gabriel, you said that we need parents to testify, right?" she asked me. I nodded. "Well, I want to make sure that I get to speak.

I want to be able to tell my story. I want to tell it right to the commissioner." Her voice, usually light and friendly, had a serious tone I hadn't heard before. "He needs to know what is happening to our community."

"Okay Lourdes, you're in," I told her. "You'll be the first parent to testify."

JUMP-STARTING OUR DEMOCRACY

Most Americans today aren't very optimistic about the future of our democracy. Like the women gathered in the basement, and Lourdes living in her lead contaminated home, people have become resigned to believing that they don't have much of a role to play in determining the direction of events in their neighborhood, their city, their state, and their country.

On the face of it, Lourdes would seem an unlikely candidate to become involved in civic affairs. She was undocumented, spoke little English, and had received only a grade school level education in Mexico. She knew very little about the laws and regulations of New York City and had been told by the landlord that she would be deported if she complained about her poor housing conditions. Taking these obstacles into account, it is understandable that she had serious reservations about becoming involved in any way.

Yet she did become involved. In the space of two months she went from someone who was afraid to make a phone call to an individual who was eager to speak about her experiences directly to the commissioner of health in front of a crowd of hundreds. She had decided that she wanted to take a stand for the health of neighborhood children, and through this decision she found herself taking on new roles and exposing herself to previously unthinkable activities. She had determined that she had the right to influence what was going on in her neighborhood.

This book is about how we can jump-start our democracy

through the practice of community organizing. It's about unearthing inspiring stories of struggle from the past and linking them to the present. It's about developing leaders like Lourdes and encouraging them to become neighborhood activists. Most of all, it's about recruiting formerly inactive, often cynical people to play their part in our unfolding democratic experiment.

———————

Even an observer with the rosiest of glasses has to conclude that our democratic experiment is in need of a dramatic jump-start. Voter turnout—that most basic barometer of political engagement—remains low. At the highest electoral level, presidential elections, just over half of American citizens usually take the time to vote; many have problems even identifying the presidential candidates. Disengagement in the political process has become routine, normal.

Democratic societies cannot exist among vast inequalities of wealth, and here, too, America faces a serious crisis. Our country has never before been in such a lopsided mess, with the top 0.5 percent of Americans holding the same amount of wealth as the bottom 42 percent.[2] In 1980, CEOs made 45 times more than their average worker; today this imbalance has increased tenfold, with CEOs making 458 times as much. As Holly Sklar, Laryssa Mykyta, and Susan Wefald document in their book *Raise the Floor,* "The gap between CEOs and minimum wage workers has become a grand canyon. In 1980, CEOs made as much as 97 minimum wage workers. In 2000, they made as much as 1,223 minimum wage workers."[3]

This inequality, bad enough in terms of the fulfillment of simple material needs, gets translated into the political arena in ways that undermine our democratic pretensions. Just running for most political offices requires a substantial amount of money; those who donate the most are thanked with special access and influence. The CEO making 1,223 times more money than the minimum-wage worker gets to flex his or her "democratic" muscles, while others unfamiliar with largesse find themselves shut out of the political process.

Finally, a vibrant democracy depends upon a strong civil society, where people regularly work with others in pursuit of common goals. We've gone from a country characterized by the presence of robust civic organizations—as Alexis de Tocqueville observed nearly two hundred years ago—to one where many people have essentially abandoned all organized activity. When people do not get the chance to work together, they fail to learn about the many common needs and desires that run deep in the veins of ordinary Americans. Without such collective interaction, our democracy is ultimately doomed—no matter how dramatically other indicators of a healthy democracy, like voter turnout, may increase.

Taken together, these three trends—anemic political participation, increasing inequality, and isolation—indicate a troubling democracy gap.

The most important question that this book attempts to answer is how best to resolve our democracy gap. How do we move uninvolved people to become active? How do we start tackling such dramatic inequality? How do we get people to stop "bowling alone," to borrow the title of Robert Putnam's famous book, and start cooperating and collaborating to pursue common interests?

We hear one answer over and over again: vote. Vote, vote, vote. If only we voted more, PhDs in political science like to remind us, many of the problems outlined above would be solved. In part, I agree. But I also can't help noticing something else: platitudes about civic duty and participation have not proven effective in activating people. Like the war on drugs, the more we preach, the worse the results seem to be. Many people appear to agree with the cynical bumper sticker that reads, "If voting solved anything, they'd make it illegal."

What follows is a controversial idea, but one that I think is nonetheless correct: calling people to vote is not the answer to our democratic crisis. The truth is, if we want to see our democracy restored, it's going to take a lot more than the simple vote—and it's not the vote that will bring unengaged people in.

From my experiences as an organizer, I've found that people are generally not initially motivated to become involved in political activities due to a desire to vote for one party or another. Poor and working-class communities all have a long history of placing their hopes in grand promises made by politicians and then feeling they've been bamboozled. They've heard lofty speeches full of promises come campaign time, then seen those same leaders ignore them once elected. People have become disengaged from political activity largely because their experiences have resulted in well earned cynicism.

Cynical people who have lost hope need to be able to find themselves in situations where their hope can be restored. They need to feel a new sense of their own power, of collective engagement, of concrete wins and tangible targets. Voting—the process of traveling to a polling booth and stepping inside a room to poke a hole in a ballot for a representative one has never met—does none of the above.

It's time that we do more than simply encourage people to vote. This book is about calling radicals out to the front lines—where they are needed most—to work as grassroots organizers and develop leaders in poor and working-class communities who can tackle critical issues such as affordable housing, health care, industrial pollution, and living wages. In the process, we can help others learn that what made this country great was not powerful politicians or massive multinational corporations, but ordinary people, like members of the WPC, who banded together to demand change.

Organizers are able to facilitate such change because, as we'll see in this book, the tactics they rely upon are uniquely positioned to spark a democratic revival. Organizers spend hours knocking on doors to engage isolated people and support them as they become leaders. They run campaigns that are informed and directed by those actually affected by the issues being worked on.

They frequently bypass formal political channels by taking direct action that ends up allowing "ordinary" residents the ability to feel their own power. And they help people think through complicated situations by engaging them in political education and conducting research that can formulate new policies that get to the root of problems instead of simply "hacking away at the branches," as Henry David Thoreau put it so elegantly in *Walden*.

Initial involvement in the organizing activities described above should lead, of course, to an increase in formal political participation such as voting—but more as an ongoing expression of people's sense that they have a right to be heard and not as a stand-alone activity that exhausts any other possibilities. Though voting is important, we have come to a point in our society where poor and working-class people are overwhelmingly skeptical about their political system—and immigrant communities, who might not yet have the ability to vote, are locked out entirely. We have to go beyond electoral politics if we want to turn people on to political activity, and the immediacy of organizing provides a perfect program. Organizing teaches people that they don't have to go through the formal channels of participation, which many have determined to be meaningless. Instead, we can chart our own course and take direct action to force the powerful to do what we wish, when they'd rather we just sit back and grant them a blank check once elected.

ORGANIZERS AS DEMOCRACY "SCOUTS"

A scout in sports is someone whose job it is to discover young and unknown talent. Each year in the United States, many scouts from professional teams travel around the world, from China to the Dominican Republic, hoping to find the next big star—a local phenomenon with an uncanny ability to hit a baseball, shoot a basketball, or kick a soccer ball.

For relatively trivial talents, we invest millions of dollars. But for issues of much greater importance, like scouting out inactive citizens and encouraging them to become involved, our investment is paltry. Though we do have certain circumscribed arenas where people are scouted, such as elite high schools and universities, these are geared toward those already accustomed to wielding power and influence. For the majority of Americans, struggling to make ends meet and unfamiliar with the halls of privilege, there are no democracy scouts within sight.

Unless one believes that somehow individuals born into privilege are better positioned to be democratic citizens, we've got a problem: millions of people are falling through the leadership cracks. In just four years working in one section of Brooklyn and conducting aggressive outreach, our organizers discovered dozens of individuals like Lourdes who have now been given the training and support needed to become engaged democratic citizens (even when they aren't, technically, "citizens"). Without having organizers go out and be democracy scouts, however, these people might never have learned the extent of what they had within them and definitely wouldn't have contributed to the many victories that we have accomplished.

Community organizing is our best bet for restoring our democracy because it recognizes that overcoming the hopelessness Americans feel cannot be accomplished alone. As democracy scouts, our job is to discover leaders and quickly bring them into contact with each other. To overcome hopelessness requires respectful interaction, a restoration of faith, the creation of a community where people are able to see themselves in a new light.

In Barbara Kingsolver's novel *Animal Dreams,* a young woman named Hallie travels to Nicaragua to support the Sandinista revolution and writes a letter to her older sister, Codi, explaining her developing philosophy:

> *Codi, here's what I've decided: the very least you can do*
> *in your life is to figure out what you hope for. And the*

*most you can do is live inside that hope. Not admire it
from a distance but live right in it, under its roof.*[4]

These words capture a key dimension of community organizing. Beyond the political demands and policy changes, at its heart organizing is about the many personal transformations that, when taken together, fuel every successful social movement. It takes courage to live in hope, to go out into the world and challenge the status quo. But this entrance into action can only occur when we construct a safe roof under which hope can develop. Lourdes found this safe roof in our group of parents—many undocumented immigrants like herself—who were determined to take a stand to protect the children of their neighborhood. Organizers, therefore, need to bring folks together so they can offer support and solidarity as they work together against what might initially appear to be long odds. This process is, in the deepest sense of the word, countercultural, and it is what enables a new feeling of promise to develop among people who previously thought of themselves as powerless.

THE MYTH OF DEMOCRATIC APATHY

When dealing with democracy, the question of apathy inevitably emerges. Especially in political science circles, academics strive to understand why citizens become apathetic once democracy is "reached." After years of struggle against unjust rule, it seems that when democracy is finally "achieved," people just stop caring. Numerous studies have been undertaken trying to comprehend this paradox of modern democracies.

Seemingly making matters worse for organizers in low-income communities is that it is the poor who have the lowest voting turnout, a fact that suggests to some that they care the least about democracy. But while I found many who seemed indifferent to democracy in theory, I discovered that these were people who were passionately interested in democracy as it related to their lives, their families, their communities—and to a much deeper degree than many of the political science students I knew in college.

This interest, however, was rarely defined as an interest in "democracy" as some sort of abstract political theory. It was instead stated in a myriad of practical applications: "Our kids get lead poisoning because the politicians don't care about poor Mexicans," or "How do they expect us to afford these rents when we hardly get paid for the work we do?" It was stated, above all, with anger at a system that ensured that people far removed from the problems they themselves experienced were calling all the shots and that they were expected to grin and bear it.

For others it is not a question of their interest but of confidence. It takes a certain amount of hubris to believe that things can change, that ordinary people can make the changes themselves, and then to risk failure by taking action and seeing what happens. Once community members became more confident, both individually and collectively, what might have been "apathy" (more often inaction fueled by feelings of powerlessness) evaporated instantly. Indeed, who has time to be apathetic when they've got things to accomplish?

This leads to another critical lesson that aspiring community organizers should remember: people do not become apathetic about democracy when it is defined as the ability to influence decisions that affect one's life. It seems to me that wanting to influence events that affect us—based on my personal experiences as well as the observations of others—is hardwired into us as a part of the human condition. In fact, the only time I hear people speak about apathy is when they're citing its presence in others. It becomes an easy way to write off millions of people without actually engaging them.

Instead of sitting around and bemoaning the "apathy" of others, organizers go out and readily discover that people do want to get involved in issues they care about. Perhaps they aren't enthralled with specific political programs that experts have designed for their stamp of approval or with approved political candidates (a judgment that reflects poorly on the candidates, not "apathetic" citizens). But my experiences in organizing have taught me that all the gibberish about apathy dissolves quite quickly when people are given the skills, training, and support needed to effect change.

CALLING ALL RADICALS:
The Challenge of Organizing, the Promise of Democracy

Democracy, as the political science professor C. Douglas Lummis writes, still has a magical ring:

> *When the word is used in the right place, at the right moment, it is fresh, clear, and true. It is not out of habit or nostalgia that we continue to use it, but because there are times when no other word can say what has to be said. And though the history of its use is a history of hypocrisy and betrayal, democracy is somehow still a virginal political idea. Understood radically, it contains a promise yet to be fulfilled.*[5]

In every neighborhood across the United States there are promises yet to be fulfilled. There are leaders waiting to emerge who have never been told that they have the ability to lead; victories waiting to be had where fights seem hopeless and dreams nonexistent; latent power to be built in areas long abused.

These future struggles are not regularly advertised in the lives of Americans. Instead, we grow up often without even knowing that such struggles exist, inheriting goals that have to do with personal aggrandizement, unthinking educational advancement, and financial fulfillment. Our lives become ruled by largely meaningless acronyms such as GPAs and SATs.

This book offers a different vision for Americans—especially the young Americans who will ultimately decide the direction of our country—illuminating an option that many might not know about. I have found that stepping outside the academic and corporate rat races reveals a very different world, one where people are faced not with the pressure to score perfect GREs but with the tasks of finding enough money to pay rent and afford health care and of working for a more democratic society. I have found spending my time in this other environment to be far more meaningful and fulfilling. I suspect many others will as well.

This book is a manual outlining one way we can jump-start this revival, discussing and analyzing the basic tactics of community organizing—with real-life examples from my experiences in Brooklyn and from veteran organizers who've been on the front lines for decades. I assume you agree, having picked up this book, that our country is in urgent need of a democratic revival, but picking up this book is only the beginning of the journey. Readers will find at the end of the book a comprehensive resource guide to groups that train and employ community organizers across the country—from the labor movement and the environment to immigrant rights and prison reform—so that when finished, one can put this book down and jump right into the field of social justice work. For if we do agree that we need more democracy in this country right now (when haven't we?), then we need more democracy builders. We need more community organizers.

Chapter 1

PLEASE REMOVE YOUR HAT BEFORE WE EVICT YOU:
Changing the System through Community Organizing

Our problems stem from our acceptance of this filthy, rotten system.
—Dorothy Day

I met Dolores at one of the legal clinics we held for tenants. She had signed a court paper forcing her to pay $4,000 back rent in a month—an impossible agreement that the landlord's attorney knew couldn't be achieved. Six months earlier, one of her daughters had experienced a medical emergency, and without health care Dolores had depleted her savings account for the necessary treatment. With only a tenuous grasp of English and four children to care for, Dolores had a court date for the following day. I asked her if she had any of the money she owed.

"No, nothing," she answered in Spanish. "I knew I would get

in trouble. I knew I didn't have enough money. But what could I do? She needed the medicine." Still, she was hopeful that the judge, a female, would understand her predicament and grant her more time. "If you come with me tomorrow we can tell the judge that I have my children and nowhere to go," she insisted. "I just need a little more time to get the money."

I had no such faith in the compassion of housing court judges, female or otherwise. "Dolores, I don't think the judge is going to give you more time, unless you can show how you will pay the money. Even if the judge is a woman, she won't try to help you. I'll go with you, but I don't think I can do much."

"Just a week or two is all I need. A little extension." She wanted to hear something encouraging from me, but I couldn't bring myself to lie. Only a few months into the job, and I already had a pretty clear sense of what usually happened at housing court.

"I hope so," I replied, doing my best to adopt a comforting voice. "But it's going to be tough. I'll be in court at nine-thirty AM. Make sure not to be late—that's one thing that can really piss off judges."

I met Dolores the next day while waiting in line to pass through the court's security screeners in front of Brooklyn's Housing Court, a depressing gray building on a depressing gray day. She was dressed in a formal black suit, complete with a beige hat and matching gloves. Obviously nervous, she was unable to stand still in the line and instead paced up and down the sidewalk while I held our spot. Eventually we made it inside, walked up to the fourth floor, and sat down on the uncomfortable wooden benches in the room where her case was going to be held. Once seated, I spent thirty minutes staring at walls and stamping out a foot threatening to fall asleep, until the judge finally entered. She was young, thin, and walked with an exaggerated military cadence. After striding to her chair, she whisked her hair back behind her ears and began to finger through the papers in front of her. We, unfortunately, were first.

The judge barked out the names of the parties, not bothering to even look up and put some faces to the names whose fate she now held in her hands. "Take a seat in front of the stand." The judge finally looked up at Dolores. "And please remove your hat immediately—you can't be wearing a hat in this courtroom!" The judge's eyes were ablaze at this insult to her profession. Dolores blushed deeply and quickly pulled her hat off, fingering it in her trembling hands.

I had followed Dolores forward to the table. My heart beat fast; I had no idea how these situations proceeded. I learned quickly enough.

"Who are you?" the judge barked again, this time staring at me.

"I'm an organizer at the Pratt Area Community Council," I answered, suddenly feeling the extent of my insignificance. "I've been working with Dolores on her case."

I could see the judge was unimpressed. "If you're not an attorney you need to sit back down. Only lawyers can represent tenants here."

I wasn't sure if this was exactly true. "But I'm an advocate, and I've been working with Dolores and told her I'd be able to at least sit next to her and explain—"

"You need to sit down!" she yelled. I hesitated, caught off guard by the volume of her voice. "You are not an attorney, so you cannot be up here! Sit down now!" I was convinced and retreated to the wooden benches. Squeezing myself into a spot between two families in the third row, I was now just another observer of this experiment in courtroom justice.

Dolores and I had gone over some different negotiation strategies, though I didn't hold out much hope that they'd be effective. She had an emergency grant pending, which would cover half the amount owed, and then she could push for a payment plan for the difference. She did work full-time, and though her bills and rent immediately swallowed up her checks, the fact that she was gainfully employed could—theoretically—allow the judge to grant her more time.

"It says here you owe four thousand dollars," the judge barked, signaling, I figured, that the trial had now begun. "Is this true?" she asked—or more accurately—again barked. She seemed able to communicate only through bark, as if a more civil tone would somehow disgrace the courtroom.

"Yes, your honor, I do owe money. But I have put in application—"

"Do you have the four thousand dollars with you?" the judge interrupted.

"No, not here. But I put in application—"

"You don't have any money with you?" The judge was determined to limit Dolores's answers to single sentences.

"No, but—"

"Then I'm sorry, but this is too much money to be owed. Do you have a job, source of income?"

"Yes, your honor. But it's hard when I never get enough to make payments. Now I have put in application. I able to—"

Dolores was again guilty of trying to speak in consecutive sentences. "Look, it says that you owed money before, too. You don't have anything with you, and you don't have any way to pay it. I have no choice. Five days to move. That gives you a little more time, but it is all I can do."

Dolores was desperate. "Judge, I have four children. I get the—"

"I'm sorry, the decision has already been made. The case is over."

Dolores stood up slowly, turned around, and looked at me. I didn't know what to do, so just waved to signal that we should get out of the courtroom.

On the street outside the courthouse we spoke briefly, but there was not much to say. Dolores left to catch the bus, fighting back tears. I began my walk back to the office, defeated.

THE "PEOPLE'S HOUSING UNIT"

The last straw came when a chunk of the ceiling collapsed on Otilia's ten-year-old daughter, knocking her unconscious. The landlord of her six-unit building had stopped doing any repairs some months ago, and constant leaks had caused severe water damage to the walls and ceilings in each apartment. One afternoon the ceiling gave way in Otilia's apartment and landed on top of her daughter's head. The tenants were ready to fight back.

We helped the six families file a collective lawsuit in housing court against the landlord, listing all of the violations that existed. However, when the tenants called the next day to schedule the inspections, the court's phone lines were busy. The following day we again spent hours attempting to get through but still were unsuccessful. Finally, on the third day someone picked up the phone but told the tenants that an inspector wouldn't be available until after the court date, which would mean that the families would have to adjourn the case and could be waiting for months before any repairs commenced.

That evening I met with the tenants to discuss possible courses of action. Some of them, convinced that there was nothing to do, were resigned to waiting until the next court date. Others argued in favor of staging a protest in front of the landlord's office. But Otilia had a brilliant idea: we could form a guerrilla housing inspection team. If the city couldn't be bothered to help tenants with emergency housing situations, then why not hold an event to challenge not only the landlord but the entire ineffectual code enforcement system that forced tenants to live in dangerous housing? And why not invite the media?

Right then and there we formed the "People's Housing Unit." I went out and bought a few jumpsuits and created official inspection forms. With some handmade patches stitched onto the uniforms, we sent out a press release offering to give the media tours of the building.

The next day we found two newspaper reporters and four television camera crews lined up outside the building. They followed the tenants and inspection team as we went from apartment to apartment, cataloguing such violations as busted water pipes, growing centers of mold, infestations of rats and cockroaches, and constant leaks and gaping holes in the bathrooms. As the inspections took place, tenant leaders spoke to the media about the need to beef up the city's code enforcement division and advocated for pending citywide legislation that would make the city's housing agency more effective in documenting and correcting violations.

Our event prompted rapid agency response: that very evening, city inspectors visited the building and did a thorough inspection of every unit, finding ninety violations. The city's housing agency issued a public apology (a first!) that was featured in a prominent newspaper the following day. The landlord, whose building was suddenly featured on many media outlets, stopped by our office and made a commitment to complete the work quickly—but we decided that given his previous inattention, we needed a court order to guarantee results. When we returned to court, we had a violation printout as evidence, and the judge ordered the landlord to make the repairs quickly or face severe financial penalties.

Two weeks later, many of the major hazards had been fixed. We had originally met the tenants and provided them with a service (legal advice and advocacy in housing court) and then gone on to work with the residents to organize a challenge to both the landlord and the city's ineffectual code enforcement system. In the process, the tenants learned that they could play a key role in solving their own problems, and this initial involvement led them to become active members in future campaigns.

A SIMPLE DEFINITION OF COMMUNITY ORGANIZING:
People Working Together to Get Things Done

Though the practice of organizing relies upon many different tactics and is constantly adapting to new situations, at its core is a simple concept. As longtime organizer Si Kahn writes, "Organizing is people working together to get things done":

Let's say you're fed up with the high prices and poor quality that you get at your neighborhood supermarket. Now, you could try to do something about it yourself. You could go to the manager and say, "If you don't straighten up, I'm not going to shop here anymore." You could write letters to the newspaper complaining about the food. You could write to the president of the chain. But they're not going to pay much attention to you. If you're just one person they don't really care whether you shop at the store or not.[1]

Alone, the problems that people face can seem overwhelming. Acting alone to fix them, people are usually powerless—unless, of course, they've got money that they can translate into results. But ordinary and isolated citizens, like Dolores in housing court, are forced to fend for themselves in the face of hostile institutions and agencies. As individuals they have little power to alter their situations and don't stand much of a chance.

When people come together and act on common interests, however, the power that they hold is revealed. Part of an organizer's job is to encourage people to believe that they hold such a power, which the tenants of the slumlord realized after forming the "People's Housing Unit." Today these families are living in newly rehabilitated housing, yet there are undoubtedly thousands of buildings across our country where tenants are still living in equally treacherous conditions. Perhaps some of the tenants are making individual phone calls to their landlords, asking for repairs. Perhaps others have long given up. But one thing is certain: Were they to organize collectively and take action, whether by going on rent strike or demonstrating in front of their landlord's home, they'd find a latent power lurking just below the surface. And they'd probably find the process of becoming public actors enjoyable, maybe even addictive.

ORGANIZING AND BUILDING POWER

This building of power is a critical component of organizing. As Michael Gecan writes in *Going Public*, which recounts the lessons he learned as an organizer with East Brooklyn Congregations, power is the answer to most community problems:

> *When we are called by the neighborhood or religious leaders of a city, we tell them that we won't come to solve a housing problem or an educational problem or a low-wage problem. No, we say we will try to help them solve a more fundamental problem—a power problem. No matter how terrible the conditions may be and no matter how intense the current crisis, we will spend a year or two or three with them not addressing these immediate and important issues and concerns. We'll use that time to build the organization and to develop a firm base of power, so that the group will someday have the punch and impact needed to instigate and preserve lasting change.*[2]

For people not familiar with organizing, this emphasis on building power is probably the most overlooked aspect of what community organizers do. Instead, many think of "organizers" as people who simply give out lots of information or who make endless phone calls to announce random rallies and demonstrations. Though organizers may at times do such activities, the ultimate goal of this work must always focus on building power. This power, which is developed by linking people together and pursuing direct action campaigns, is what enables communities to push through policies and create real change. One thousand educational workshops or community-building activities might help bring people together, but without a subsequent campaign of action with specific demands directed at specific targets, it's not yet organizing.

This emphasis on building power may make some feel uncomfortable; after all, people with power are what we're fighting, right? But it is helpful to remember that the Spanish word for power, *poder*, also has a second meaning: "to be able to do something." In this way, power is simply the ability to act and to have influence over what we want to see happen. Either the fabulously wealthy and politically connected will act with impunity, or poor and working-class communities will hold them accountable with their own power, achieved through collective action. In neighborhoods where little power currently exists, effective organizers facilitate a transformation so that people have the confidence and ability to act collectively, to build power.

PROGRESS EMERGES FROM CONFLICT AND TENSION

In organizing, conflict and tension play key roles. Changes that we seek will not come about in the form of gifts from above but from struggles from the grass roots. It has always been this way in the past. It will always be this way in the future.

If we're not creating conflict and tension, something is amiss. There is a tendency to view progress as a "natural" development that occurs when two sides come together spontaneously and find common ground. But this is a highly inaccurate picture; indeed, victories by groups of ordinary Americans occur only after a fight, when the powerful—whether politicians, agency heads, or multinational corporations—realize they are getting beaten and come to the table and make concessions. Only then, when the fight is won, do the powerful emerge as "allies" who do their best to position themselves as having been working for the same goals all along. That, of course, is fine: when our targets do what we want, they do become our allies and are due all of the positive PR they can squeeze out of their defeat.

But we should be clear: progress emerges from conflict. As the legendary organizer Saul Alinsky writes, to pretend otherwise is just plain foolish: "Change means movement. Movement means friction. Only in the frictionless vacuum of a nonexistent abstract world can movement or change occur without that abrasive friction of conflict."[3]

Alinsky knew what all organizers soon learn: our targets will not roll over. Organizers work to develop groups that are affected by problems and take action to win meaningful change. Whatever the changes sought, be they higher fines for slumlords or universal health care, we will find entrenched interests that will not roll over and concede or simply respond to our demands because they are "correct." They will respond when we fight power with power and they decide that the costs of fighting us outweigh the benefits of conceding to our demands.

If organizers do not understand this simple fact, they may end up in symbolic situations of power where they win nothing concrete but spend a lot of time discussing their ideas with opponents in arenas such as "advisory" committees created by those who are just siphoning off precious energy into unproductive channels. As Noam Chomsky writes:

> There's nothing that elites like better than saying, "Oh come convince me." That stops you from organizing, and getting people involved, and causing disruption, because now you're talking to some elite smart guy—and you can do that forever: any argument you can give in favor of it, he can give an argument against it, and it just keeps going . . . if you're getting invited into elite circles, chances are very strong that you're doing something wrong, for very simple reasons. Why should they have any respect for people who are trying to undermine their power? It doesn't make any sense.[4]

Organizers, then, need to learn to live with tension and to worry when things seem to be proceeding without friction. The tension, in a phrase used frequently by Saul Alinsky, is between the world as it is and the world as it should be. When we take action to try to bring these two worlds closer together, we get conflict. And when we're effective, this conflict leads to victory, which makes our society a tad more humane by responding to the needs of ordinary Americans.

PULLING THE BABIES FROM THE RIVER:
Understanding the Difference between
Community Organizing, Social Service, and Advocacy

Understanding that organizing is about people acting together to get what they want and build power, and acknowledging that this work will always generate tension and conflict, makes it easier to differentiate organizing from other forms of nonprofit work. Though many people lump organizing, social service, and advocacy together, important philosophical and practical differences exist. Understanding these differences is critical to understanding whether one actually wants to become a community organizer.

Linda Stout, in *Bridging the Class Divide,* cites a quotation from an activist that outlines nicely the core difference in emphasis between community organizers and service providers: "[People] are so busy trying to pull the babies that are drowning out of the river that they never stop to go to the head of the river to see who's throwing them in."[5]

Organizing is about working with people and developing leaders who can go to the head of the river and directly challenge the "baby throwers." Using this metaphor, Dolores was drowning and had been thrown into the river by a landlord and judge who refused to grant her more time to pay off her debt. Yet this crisis was only an outgrowth of the real problem: Dolores's daughter did not have health care, which had created the debt in the first place. And this crisis was related to another: Dolores's wages were so low that she couldn't afford to save any money, so whenever a situation emerged that forced her to dip into her limited resources, she was pushed to the brink of homelessness.

When we only provide services, we often engage in a desperate project of pulling drowning babies from the river. When I helped Dolores go over her legal options and prepare the best case she had, I was providing a service. It was an important service, to be sure, and when we succeed in providing critical services, the individual victories are real. But providing services does nothing to ensure that other people, who may never walk through our doors, aren't being tossed into the river as well. This is because service providers exist not to challenge the system that has made their job necessary in the first place but to enable clients to maneuver as best they can through a broken system. Service providers are experts at working within the system but are generally not allowed (or even able—since they have such heavy caseloads) to agitate for systemic change. Their existence legitimizes the system and does little to get at the root of problems.*

Providing services also does little to engage people and does nothing to develop leadership among those affected by institutional dysfunction. Usually when we provide a service, someone receives assistance with their problem and then goes on their way. In terms of helping people with their immediate issues, it can be an effective arrangement (though it obviously wasn't for Dolores).

---

* My point here is not to disparage social workers (my mom is a social worker, after all, and a damn fine one). I simply want to make two separate points: social workers perform necessary work, but they also perform work that unavoidably condones the current arrangement that has forced their services to be necessary. They may be radical in temperament, but their relationships with clients revolve around giving out information and guiding people through bureaucracies so that their needs can be met. The legitimacy of the institutions that force such maneuvering, due to the nature of their work, is not usually on the agenda.

But it does not, as is critical to organizing, create a base of members who can get beyond a reactive position. It does not allow people to do anything except follow directions, which is not generally an empowering experience.

Advocacy is different from both social services and organizing. A helpful way to think about advocates is to think about the role of attorneys. Attorneys have clients who come to them for assistance; integral to this relationship is the concept that the attorney has special information that the client doesn't and can therefore speak "for" the client effectively. Clients rely on advocates to represent their interests and usually play a minimal role themselves in the process.

Many advocacy organizations do great work—my point is not to criticize them—but if they do only advocacy, then their work is fundamentally different from organizing. Many homeless advocacy groups, for example, are very effective. They are made up of people who aren't homeless and usually haven't ever experienced being homeless but who believe that housing is a human right to be enjoyed by all. They study the issue, speak out about injustice, and frequently represent homeless people in legal cases.

But a community organizing group tackling the problem of homelessness would focus its energy toward developing leaders within the homeless community itself who can play a role in determining solutions. These leaders could then design campaigns with a direct action component that allowed them to become actual actors, not simply clients. It may seem like a subtle difference, but it is crucial. Community organizing is about developing leaders who are actually affected by the issues being confronted, so that they can advocate for themselves collectively to redress systemic problems. Neither service providers nor advocates have as their core emphasis the development of leaders among affected communities, and so neither are able to change the power disparity that has caused the problem in the first place.

COMBINING SERVICES, ADVOCACY, AND ORGANIZING

Observing the differences between service provision, advocacy, and organizing doesn't mean that we can't successfully combine them at times, but it does mean that we have to be conscious of the tensions and potential pitfalls that exist when we do. Many organizers straddle all three worlds, as I did in Brooklyn. Whether in the tenant movement, welfare rights movement, or many others, organizers often perform a service-provider function, advocacy function, and a commitment to organizing for change. Organizers frequently first meet individuals who are directly affected by specific problems, and though they attempt to help them with their individual cases, they also put much energy toward developing leaders who can challenge the system. The development of leaders who identify an institutional problem and take action to correct it is organizing. Providing services to people allows an organizer to know the system and its flaws well, but it is not organizing.

The bottom line is that providing services does not lead inevitably—as it may seem with the "People's Housing Unit" example—to organizing. This is for a variety of reasons, as outlined by veteran organizer Rinku Sen:

> Some organizers, including myself, fantasize that running services will bring the people most affected right to our doorstep, identified and available to be organized. There are three problems with this fantasy. First, people go to service providers for different reasons than they go to a political organization. This is not to say that none of the people in a soup line or waiting for legal services are interested in organizing, but they might not be acting on that interest at that moment. Second, service provision is easier to conduct than organizing; organizing is

more demanding because you actually have to get people
to do something. . . . Third, service provision is far easier
to fund than organizing.[6]

The Industrial Areas Foundation (IAF), founded by Alinsky in 1940, has what it calls an "Iron Rule": "Never, never do for others what they can do for themselves." This principle comes from the belief that what is most important is not simply helping individuals with their problems but developing people's own abilities to solve problems themselves. Service providers and advocates are almost entirely in the business of doing "for" others, and once an organization heads down this path, the overwhelming tendency is to drop the organizing component. This is due, above all, to the fact that the need for services appears more immediate and concrete and can easily push out any space for organizing—whose practices such as leadership development demand a substantial investment of time and will not necessarily create rapid results.

Not only does providing services not naturally lead to leadership development, but it also might undercut organizing efforts. A thorough and lucid exploration of the potential conflicts between service provision and organizing is found in Jennifer Gordon's book *Suburban Sweatshops*. Gordon, who founded the Workplace Project in 1992 to organize immigrant day laborers on Long Island, writes candidly about the effects of holding legal clinics for workers while also attempting to organize for power. Though a legal clinic might seem like the perfect way to attract and retain dedicated leaders, Gordon at times found otherwise:

> *[O]nce the clinic won their lawsuit and they received*
> *their money, these workers frequently left to find other*
> *jobs (if they had not already been fired). The rest of the*
> *workers, who would have benefited from their leadership*
> *had they stayed, were left to suffer. Such workers also*
> *rarely remained active in the Workplace Project after their*

> *cases were resolved. By "paying off" the bravest and more*
> *determined workers with a settlement or an award, the*
> *Workplace Project's legal program was unwittingly*
> *playing the role of the employer who decapitates an*
> *organizing effort by making a deal with its leaders.*[7]

Indeed, some groups that combine organizing with legal advocacy have found it necessary to develop intraorganizational systems to emphasize the primacy of organizing. Make the Road by Walking, an innovative and rapidly growing grassroots organization in the Bushwick section of Brooklyn—its current membership stands at twenty-three hundred—has become sophisticated in its approach. "We make sure that when a new person comes into our office off the street, the first person they talk to is an organizer," explains Make the Road's codirector Andrew Friedman. Though many people walk through the doors looking for individual assistance, they are told that services, lawsuits, and the like are only one aspect of the organization's work. An organizer explains the need to build power and that without organizing, the legal path isn't terribly effective at creating systemic change.

In addition, if a person wants legal assistance, she must become a dues paying member of Make the Road and attend a membership orientation. After this occurs, an organizer can refer the new member to the appropriate lawyer or paralegal, and she will sign a retainer agreeing that she will remain active within the organization for the duration of the suit, defined by participating in at least two actions a month—anything from attending a committee meeting to a protest—or that she may pay a fee for the legal services she receives. "It's a way of saying that they're in this with us together," explains Friedman. "It's a commitment for the organization to take these cases, and so we want to make sure that they're making a commitment as well. We want them to feel ownership."

When a case promises to be especially drawn out and will demand substantial organizing to pressure the target, the group of affected workers presents their problems to the workplace committee. Friedman describes the process:

> If a group of three people from a factory comes in and asks the committee to take up the case as a campaign, the committee will often say: "Okay, but not before you come back here with ten more workers." The committee members know how much work it will take to win the case—actions at the factory and such—and they want to make sure it's going to be worth their time and that the workers are really serious about this.

Union organizing is one area where service provision and advocacy play negligible roles. But in most neighborhood-based groups, an organizer will be balancing the three tasks, and if an organization does not have a strong commitment to organizing and clearly understands the differences between organizing and service provision, it will naturally focus on the latter and abandon the former. Therefore many of the organizations that state that they engage in "organizing" are in reality simply providing services and do not actually have a base of members who participate in deciding the issues and taking collective action. For this reason, when interviewing for positions advertised as "community organizers," individuals should do their research to determine exactly what type of work the organization defines as "organizing." I know many people aspiring to become organizers who have landed "organizing" positions that in fact are social service jobs and have ended up frustrated and discouraged.

———

Service providers and advocates often share the same values as community organizers. Yet the work they do differs greatly. While social service agencies and advocacy groups work hard to represent the interests of their clients, they generally do so within the existing framework that has caused the problem in the first place. When—despite their best efforts—the system fails their clients, the game is up. Their job is done; they move on to another client.

But when organizers find that the system doesn't work and people become frustrated by inhumane institutions, unaccountable politicians, or unresponsive corporations, the fight is not over. We've got a tactic up our sleeve, a tactic that has played a critical role in every major accomplishment by progressive forces in our country. That tactic, to which we now turn our attention, is direct action.

Chapter 2

A WORD OF ENTHUSIASM:
Direct Action Gets the Goods!

> *The costs of running for office are enormous for average people in terms*
> *of time and money, and the impediments to change built into the*
> *legislative process make it very hard to sustain a pressure-group*
> *coalition or legislative social movement that does not have a*
> *great amount of money and patience. But if average people*
> *have very little power through voting or lobbying . . .*
> *they do have power when they disrupt the system.*
> —William Dunhoff, *The Power Elite and the State*[1]

> *Those who profess to favor freedom, and yet depreciate agitation,*
> *are men who want crops without plowing up the ground.*
> —Frederick Douglass[2]

When the most powerful member of the New York City Council walked by our group demonstrating in front of a cute four-story building in Greenwich Village, he was nearly speechless with anger.

"You guys have got some real class," he sputtered, not even bothering to pause before heading through the front door. We stopped for a moment, contemplating the odd statement, but then started up our chants again: "Miller, shame / We know your name / Protecting slumlords is your game!"

The tony townhouse that we had descended upon was hosting a fund-raiser for Gifford Miller, then speaker of the New York City Council who was preparing to launch a run for the mayoral office. Every few minutes we would have to move aside as impeccably dressed individuals passed into the house, clearly upset that their chance to schmooze was being disrupted by this ragtag ensemble. Even unaffiliated people strolling by shot us looks of disgust; one woman, walking her toy poodle so that it could do its evening business, scooped the critter up in her arms and crossed the street, apparently concerned that we were prepared to bludgeon to death the local pets to prove our point.

PACC, along with other members of the New York City Coalition to End Lead Poisoning (NYCCELP), was targeting Miller because he had refused to sign on to an antilead poisoning bill that had broad support in City Council and had let a year pass without even scheduling a hearing on the proposed legislation. Miller had decided that he could ignore our group. We had decided that we could make this politically damaging for him, especially because he had aspirations to run for mayor and would need the Latino and African-American vote to do it. Since 94 percent of lead-poisoned children in the city were children of color, to appear insensitive to their needs would cast him as another aloof politician, more concerned with his big donors than regular New Yorkers. Parents of lead-poisoned children, though not in possession of the big checking accounts necessary for a formal invitation to the fund-raiser, decided to come anyway.

The *New York Times* sent a reporter to our demonstration and the next day ran a story that highlighted the charge of racism that was being levied at Miller by those affected by lead poisoning and his inaction on a bill that had such broad support. Within a few months—with increasing pressure brought on by negative press and the aggressive coalition—he came onto our side by endorsing the legislation, and in so doing became instantly transformed from an adversary to an ally.

PLAYING WITHIN THE SYSTEM:
Often Powerless by Design

A few months after we forced Miller to sign on, the City Council scheduled a public hearing on the new bill. After more than a year of being ignored, our decision to resort to direct action had resulted in damaging media coverage for Miller and a general sense from councilmembers that something had to be done to better protect children. Now it was time to work officially within the system through participating in a public hearing and stating our opinions for the record.

More than twenty parents whose children had been lead-poisoned took the day off from work to testify at the hearing. We entered the chambers of City Hall at the beginning of testimony from two City agencies, the departments of health and housing. Both were steadfastly against the new bill and both had testified at length within the past year in City Hall on the same subject. On this date the agencies' representatives were the first to testify, and they rambled on for more than four hours. As well-paid commissioners, they had not been directly affected by lead poisoning.

Parents who had intimate experience with the issue, on the other hand, were forced to sit through hours of bureaucratic testimony (many who were able to stay awake couldn't even understand a word being said, as they spoke Spanish and no translation services had been provided by the city). At the conclusion of the agencies' testimony, parents were amazed and angered when they watched the commissioners and their entourage stand up, turn around, and walk out—without bothering to listen to any other testimony. The message was clear: our voices count; your voices do not.

In the whole day of testimony, only two affected parents were able to speak, and their remarks were limited to three minutes apiece. Most of the parents took the day off from work, sat through eight hours of talk, and went home without getting a chance to contribute to the debate on an issue on which they were experts. Most of our members had no illusions about democratic platitudes; they knew that politicians would only do what we forced them to do. But when they came to testify at a "public" hearing about an issue that directly affected them, they were shut out. It was, as educators like to say, a "teachable moment."

DIRECT ACTION:
Demanding Access in Our Own Way

Direct action has a militant, robust, slightly romantic feeling about it. It sounds serious, and it is. Perhaps the best understanding of direct action comes not simply from analyzing the various forms it can take but by stepping back and outlining its philosophical core. In the final sentences of his magisterial book, *A People's History of the United States,* radical historian Howard Zinn does just that:

> Sometime in 1992, the Republican Party held a dinner to raise funds, in which individuals and corporations paid up to $400,000 to attend. A spokesman for President Bush, Marlin Fitzwater, told reporters: "It's buying access to the system, yes." When asked about people who didn't have so much money, he replied: "They have to demand access in other ways."
>
> That may have been a clue to Americans wanting real change. They would have to demand access in their own way.[3]

"Demanding access in their own way" is a good way to think about what direct action is; the term direct action usually defines organizing in the popular mind. Technically speaking, a direct action is an event where a group with a specific demand directly confronts the person (or institution—though the institution will always have a figurehead—who then becomes the target) who has the power to grant the demand. Direct action can include everything from holding rallies and walking picket lines to staging prayer vigils—even engaging in civil disobedience and risking arrest.

Direct action can be an incredibly effective tactic when used correctly. By refusing simply to play into the hands of those we oppose through frequently symbolic gestures that in no way build power for our side, we can use direct action to wake up targets and win goals that initially might seem unattainable. Who would believe, for instance, that a group of tenant organizations and other neighborhood nonprofits would be able to beat the entrenched real estate interests of New York City and pass the strongest antilead poisoning bill in the country? Or that a group of students refusing to accommodate to restaurant segregation in Greensboro, North Carolina, could ignite a spark that launched a massive sit-in movement across the South?

Behind every direct action is a simple philosophy: people have the right to make their own rules and to determine their own course of action to get what they want. Mark Toney, the former executive director of Direct Action for Rights and Equality (DARE), an organizing group in Rhode Island, exemplifies this feeling when he speaks of DARE's philosophy on introducing their organization to targets:

> When we go into an office to demand a meeting with someone that has ignored us, the person at the front desk always asks, "Well, do you have an appointment?" We answer, "No, we're DARE. We don't

> *make appointments." What can they say to that? They can't say that we're not telling the truth, can they?*

Of course, organizations have to be strategic about their use of direct action; stating that we can make our own rules doesn't mean that we're free to do whatever we want, carelessly deciding on actions without thinking about the likelihood of achieving the goals we desire. Simply reacting to everything without contemplating the ramifications will quickly lead a campaign down a dead end. Yet this idea—that we can actually make our own rules and decide our own course of action without permission from those we want to hold accountable—is at the heart of direct action.

This chapter looks at two direct actions in detail to serve as a springboard for an exploration of why direct actions work (and why at times they might not work). There are many tactics in organizing that may work in one neighborhood or among one group but are not applicable to another. But if there is one tactic that is the heart and soul of organizing—and that would be impossible to imagine organizing without—it is direct action.

GETTING ON THE CALENDAR

When PACC conducted a participatory research project that tested dozens of homes in the Bedford-Stuyvesant neighborhood of Brooklyn, we found that one third had very high lead levels (more on this in chapter 5). A week before we released the findings, we asked for a meeting with the commissioner of health, Thomas Frieden.

We were seeking a meeting to discuss the need for an early intervention policy that would be of great benefit to our members. Although medical research has shown that children experience a dramatic drop in IQ and suffer other cognitive deficiencies when they have blood lead levels below 10 micrograms per deciliter, the Department of Health usually only went out to inspect homes when their first blood lead test registered at 20 micrograms and above. Many PACC members had children with lead levels between 5 and 19 but couldn't receive any help from the agency and were concerned about further poisoning their children.

We decided to give Frieden two weeks to respond to our request for the meeting. Once the two-week deadline was up, we met with our parent leaders, many of whose children had actually been lead-poisoned, and planned a prayer vigil in front of the Department of Health's headquarters in Manhattan. The idea was to pray for the enlightenment of Commissioner Frieden on the issue and then go inside and demand a meeting. Accompanying us would be two religious leaders, one of whom who had participated in previous direct actions with us.

The morning of the vigil was oppressively hot, one of those summer days in New York City when every sane person is safely inside an air-conditioned office drinking plenty of chilled water. Our group of parents and clergy met at PACC's office, went over the plan, and then took the subway to Lower Manhattan. We had a banner, signs, a copy of the letter that had previously been sent, and plenty of children in tow.

We arrived at the headquarters sweating and gathered in a circle in front of the main entrance. After a short prayer by one of the pastors, we entered the building and lined up at the security checkpoint one has to pass through before entering the lobby. PACC organizer Hector Rivera and the clergy led the way, expecting to have to do a bit of negotiating to get into the lobby. They were greeted by a guard who seemed to have orders not to allow anyone in our group through the metal detectors upon pain of death.

"If you don't have an appointment, then I'm going to have to ask you to leave," the guard was saying for the second time.

"I'm sorry," Hector replied, "but we've come all the way from Bedford-Stuyvesant today, and we're not going to leave until someone from the Department of Health comes down here. That doesn't seem too much to ask for."

After a few more exchanges, the woman finally figured out that we really *weren't* going to leave. By now, adding some extra drama to the situation, scores of police had gathered in the lobby on the other side of the metal detectors, perhaps preparing to pummel our group if we ever did get through the security checkpoint. The guard told us that she was going to see if anyone from the Department of Health was around and retreated out of sight. She came back twenty minutes later and ushered us through the detectors, telling us to wait in the lobby for a representative to come down. Once we made it through, the group of cops that had been staring at us approached.

"You can't be demonstrating here in the lobby," the lead officer said to our group in a reprimanding tone.

I looked at our group, standing silently in front of the fifteen cops, and said, "We're not demonstrating here, any more than you guys are. We're just trying to schedule a meeting with the commissioner."

The officer glanced at our group of parents, children, and clergy and was satisfied. "Okay, you can stay here, but just make sure not to get in anyone's way."

While we waited for someone to come down, we wondered amongst ourselves why so many police had been summoned. Even in the post-9/11 environment, sending so many officers to greet our group seemed a bit extreme. In any event, I was grateful that we had brought the clergy and children along.

After five minutes, the director of communications for the agency came down from the third floor with two of her coworkers. She asked us what the trouble was. One of our core leaders, Enrique, explained that we wanted a meeting with the commissioner to discuss the lead-poisoning crisis that existed in Bedford-Stuyvesant.

"You know, it is easier to just ask us, and we'll get you on the calendar," she said. "I know that he is really concerned about the issue and I'm sure he would love to speak to you all about it."

She was doing her job, that of damage control, but we showed her our request for a meeting from two weeks ago. She apologized for the inaction and promised that we would have a meeting with the commissioner as soon as possible.

Leaving the building, one of our organizers ran into a police officer stationed outside. She learned from the cop that someone had reported that our group had sprayed mace on one of the Department of Health employees and that his team had been called to investigate the situation. This fact explained the enormous police presence that we encountered when we entered the lobby. I wondered if a group of white tourists wandering in would have been greeted with the same paranoia (our group was mostly black and Latino). Still, as we walked back to the subway station we were in high spirits, happy with the outcome of the action.

The following day the Department of Health called to schedule a meeting with the commissioner, and a few weeks later our group of parents and children were sitting down with him in an air-conditioned office to discuss our demands. We had gotten on his calendar after all: he could ignore a politely written request to meet but not a group of parents who simply showed up on his own turf. As the Industrial Workers of the World slogan enthusiastically put it years ago, "Direct action gets the goods!"

DIRECT ACTIONS ARE NOT ISOLATED EVENTS

It is important to understand that direct actions are not events that stand alone simply as impressive monuments to our ability to mobilize. Instead, a direct action is a particular tactic that is incorporated along a campaign timeline when it is needed to accomplish a goal, and what we do the next day is often just as important as the action itself. In this manner, organizing is a bit different from large-scale mobilizations that can have hundreds of thousands of participants but then disburse, regrouping a few months later at another large protest, and that might not have a specific demand.

In the above example, our ultimate goal was to force the Department of Health to adopt an early intervention program. The specific target who had the power to make this change was the commissioner of health. A first step toward our goal was to hold a face-to-face meeting with him to discuss the benefits of our proposal and to have our members state the demand directly to the target.

If the commissioner had decided to meet with us after receiving the letter, that would have been great. As organizer Mili Bonilla states, direct action is akin to an umbrella: "You put it away in the closet when you don't need it, but always in the same place, so you can get to it easily when you do."[4]

The commissioner's initial inaction made it clear that he did not feel sufficient political pressure; instead, he probably figured we were just a small group from Brooklyn that would forget about the issue when ignored. Why take time out of his busy schedule to meet with unruly parents when in all likelihood they'd just go away? He probably received dozens of letters each month asking for his attention, and we must have been pretty low on the totem pole. So we met with our members and decided on an action that needed no invitation and ended up getting what we wanted.★

★ The Department of Health never did institute an early intervention program on its own, but the City Council passed a new lead bill that required the agency to take action whenever a child tested with 15 micrograms per deciliter.

FIGHTING THE EVICTION OF MICHAEL & MILLIE

What would become our largest antieviction campaign began innocently enough with a phone call from a woman named Millie, who left her number on my voice mail and said something about the landlord playing a joke on her and her brother by asking them to leave. Skeptical about the idea that humor was somehow involved, I called her back, and we set up an appointment for her to come into the office.

The evening of the meeting Millie showed up early. "My parents bought our home in 1929," Millie began. "I was seven when we moved in. My little brother Michael was born in the home. A few years later our father died, so mom took care of the building from then on. In 1987, mom passed away, and Michael and I decided to sell the building to a family friend. We sold it for $20,000, but we spent all of the money on mom's funeral. Who knew a funeral could cost so much?"

She looked like she wanted an answer. "I had no idea, myself," I answered.

"So anyway, it cost way too much. And we sold the building to a family friend, who agreed that we could live there as long as we wanted."

"Then the friend shouldn't be able to evict you and Michael," I said. "Do you have a copy of the agreement?"

Millie rustled around in her bag and then straightened up. "Oh, you see, the friend lost the building to the bank. He would never have done anything like this to us. It's the new landlord who wants us out."

"And you've spoken to the new landlord?" I asked.

"No, not since we got the letter. He hasn't called me back. Michael tried calling, too, but he just got a recording."

"Where is Michael?" I asked, curious that the younger brother had allowed his sister to walk all the way to our office in the dark.

"He's very sick," she replied. "He can't get out of bed right now. He's got an infected leg and neurological problems. And a weak heart. This whole thing is terrible for him. He keeps waking me up in the middle of the night and asking where we'd go, how we'd be able to find a new place."

We made copies of the documents Millie had brought and told her to come to our next organizing meeting, where she could share her story with our members. We also asked her to come to our legal clinic the following week, so that an attorney from South Brooklyn Legal Services could try to sort out this mess.

Millie got up to leave. "Gabriel, we never would have let this happen if we'd known someone wanted us out. Never. But Michael and I didn't know anything about evictions or any of that. I just hope it's not too late, that we can do something."

"At least you're in good hands," I said. "We work with the best tenant lawyers and we've got a dedicated group of people here— they've worked to stop a number of evictions before. Until then, just tell Michael everything is going to be fine. No sense in making him any more worried than he already is."

"Oh no, I wouldn't think of it. He's already having heart trouble because of it. I wake up each morning and try to tell him everything will be all right. But he knows that I'm not sure, either."

At our community meeting, Millie's story galvanized our members, who organized a letter writing campaign and wanted to begin planning a direct action. We held off on the action (we still hadn't been able to find out the landlord's address) but agreed that we'd begin leafleting in front of his home as soon as we found out where he lived.

The following week we finally tracked down the landlord's residence, on a busy street called Division Avenue in the Brooklyn neighborhood of Williamsburg. Williamsburg, like many sections of New York City, boasts a diverse population, including longtime Puerto Rican and African-American residents, Hasidic Jews of the Satmar sect, and, most recently, young white hipsters. Early one weekday morning, PACC members headed over to the building with leaflets in hand. Four members stood out front, handing leaflets to people passing by, four went around the block posting the papers on signposts, and two others went inside to put them under each apartment door so that all of the landlord's neighbors would learn why we were here. Everything was going well for the first ten minutes, as Latino, Hasidic, and African-American families walking by all seemed sympathetic to the case and wished us luck. Then, while I was standing outside the apartment with Millie, talking to a Hasidic woman, a man swung the front door of the building open violently and an angry, crimson face peered out.

"What is this? What are you doing?!" he demanded.

I took a deep breath. "We are here," I said in as soft and gentle a voice as I could put together, "because this woman, Millie, might be evicted from her home of seventy-three years. The landlord lives in the building here, and so we want to let him know that we don't think he should evict Millie." There, that seemed reasonable enough.

"This landlord?" The man asked, holding up the flyer we had put under his door. "This person, at apartment 2-L?"

"Yes, that's it," Millie said.

"Well, I can't believe this!" the man bellowed. "*I* live at 2-L, and I am not the landlord of anything!"

I hadn't prepared for this.

"Now these papers, you need to get rid of them! I can't believe you're doing this to me!" He was staring directly at me.

I tried to focus on the facts as I saw them. "According to our information from the city, the landlord lives here at 2-L. Look, I've got it right here," and I pulled out a folded sheet of paper that I was suddenly immensely relieved to have brought along. The man, still fuming, looked at the paper. Yes, it did say that the landlord lived at 2-L. He calmed down a little.

"We're sorry if we made a mistake," said Frances, one of our community leaders. "This is all we have to go by. And we've got an old woman here who might be evicted, so we have to find the landlord. You don't know this person? Did he used to live here?"

I was glad that Frances was being polite. I knew the possibility existed that the man in front of us was indeed the landlord, but I didn't think we should push it. If he honestly was an innocent victim of a bureaucratic mistake, then he had good cause for being upset when suddenly every neighbor of his thought that he was evicting an elderly brother and sister he had never heard of. For now, the least we could do was give him the benefit of the doubt.

Back at the office I had a message. It was from the property manager, who had heard of our "shenanigans" and wanted us to stop. He said he would negotiate if we put an end to our games. This sounded too easy—we supposedly hadn't even targeted the right place, after all—but who were we to argue with a quick victory? I called him back and we came to an agreement: our group wouldn't do anything else, and in return Michael and Millie could remain in their homes. It sounded good to me, and we decided to speak the following day to set up a time to meet and sign some papers to make it official. It would be a great experience for our leaders to sit down across the table from the property manager and feel the power they held.

But the next day, when I called, I was told that he had changed his mind. He now wanted me to speak with his attorney on all matters. So I called the attorney, who told me that he didn't care about our little games—Michael and Millie had to get out because they had no legal right to stay. Back to square one.

We went back out, this time handing out flyers in front of the address we had discovered for the property manager's house. Again we spoke to many sympathetic people who promised to make a call in support of the threatened siblings.

This time we didn't hear from either the property manager or landlord. Wanting to explore other avenues, I called a friend who worked at the largest Hasidic organization in Williamsburg, the United Jewish Organizations (UJO). I asked her if she thought the director, Rabbi David Neiderman, could give the property manager a call and increase the pressure. After speaking with the rabbi, she found out that *his* parents had been evicted when seniors, and he was very upset that a member of his community was trying to do something similar. The rabbi then called the property manager and yelled at him, but it didn't seem to have had any effect yet. The landlord and property manager appeared to be digging in for a protracted fight.

By this time we had postponed the housing court case twice, hoping to buy enough time to find out where the landlord lived. Searching through different records, we ended up with three new addresses, but after visiting the locations, we realized that some elaborate scheming was going on. The landlord seemed to be nowhere, and the phone numbers we came up with all led in an unhelpful circle of people who denied that they had ever heard of the man. Finally, a friend and union researcher came upon an address in upstate New York, in a small town called Monsey. Doing research on Monsey, I learned that it was an enclave of Hasidic Jews. Many people I spoke to had heard of the area, yet no one had been there, even though it was only forty-five minutes away. We were, of course, concerned that we would go all the way up to the town and find it was just another fake address—so a few members and myself tried calling. Twice a woman picked up and said that she had never heard of the man. The third time, however, a child picked up, and when I asked if the landlord was there he said, innocently, "No, he is at work right now."

"But he lives there?" I asked.

"Yeah," the boy answered.

"What's that address again?"

He repeated the address we had.

Bingo.

We organized a caravan to go up to Monsey on a Sunday—a day without religious significance to Jews.★

I was a little anxious about taking our group to the town, as some people had warned me that any outsiders would be made to feel quite unwelcome—especially a group of mostly African Americans who were challenging the actions of one of their community members. Still, we discussed the issue with our members and Millie, and they all agreed that we had to go. Community leaders prepared a giant card asking the landlord to stop the eviction, and Millie put her own feelings down on a separate card that, if we were lucky enough finally to have the right house, she would personally hand over to the landlord.

Sunday morning, with a group of eight community leaders and a reporter who had heard about the campaign, we took off for Monsey. As we got closer, I expected to see the land turn into something akin to Amish country, but the landscape and inhabitants remained unchanged and looked like any other suburban setting. When we finally arrived, we found that Monsey was not at all the isolated enclave that we had expected. Right next to what looked like the beginning of the Hasidic houses were people of all races, doing normal things like hanging out in front of convenience stores. I breathed a sigh of relief.

Just a short distance from the strip malls, the road became quieter and turned residential. We came across the street we were looking for and parked our cars in a patch of dirt on the side of the road. Emboldened by the ordinariness of the neighborhood, we decided to walk a few blocks through the area. We hoped to gain

---

★ These types of details are critical to organizing. Local customs, religious beliefs, modes of dress, methods of addressing people—all must be known by organizers. To inadvertently behave insensitively to groups can be fatal to organizing efforts, and so when endeavors lead the organizer into unfamiliar territory, as I found myself with the Hasidim, doing some quick research is necessary.

people's attention and get some dialogue going about this odd group of black and white, young and old, parading by their homes on a calm weekend morning.

We got ourselves together and prepared to walk. By now eyes were peering out from front porches and behind closed windows. "Millie, you have the card, right?" Jackie Mitchell, a community leader, asked.

"Um . . ." Millie searched through her front pockets and came up empty-handed. "Ah, here it is!" she proclaimed with a smile, and we all laughed and began to walk. As we made our way down the street, people came out on to their porches and two men on bicycles who seemed to be informal security guards of some sort appeared. We reached the house we were looking for without incident and walked up a long set of steps. Millie gently knocked on the door. A young boy answered.

"Hello," Millie said. She asked if the landlord was around.

"Uh-huh. I'll get him." The boy walked down a hallway, and a few seconds later a woman emerged.

"Yes, may I help you?" she asked with undisguised hostility.

We had decided that Millie ought to be the one doing most of the talking. "Yes, we are looking for my landlord. My name is Millie Gaeta and he's trying to evict me and my brother."

The woman's face registered nothing. "I'm sorry. This person doesn't live here. You have the wrong place."

"That a lie!" shouted a member from behind me, and I decided I didn't want the situation to get out of hand.

"We're sorry if we have the wrong place," I said. "It's just that this brother and sister are in danger of being evicted, and we can't seem to find the landlord. When we looked up some records it said that he lived here."

"No, that's wrong." She didn't look like she was going to budge.

"Can we at least leave these letters for him?" I asked.

"But I almost never see him," she answered. "He just has some of his mail sent here. There's really no reason to leave him something here."

Just has his mail sent here? That was a pretty implausible story, as the groans of our group indicated, but she was doing her best to shield her husband on short notice.

I motioned to the group. "We've come all the way from Brooklyn. We can't find this man anywhere, and we can't just leave without doing anything. Can you please take these for—"

"Everything okay here?" One of the security guards had dismounted from his bike and was at the foot of the stairs. The woman answered in Yiddish, and the man appeared satisfied and biked off to a position across the street, keeping a watchful eye on the situation.

"All we are asking," pleaded Jackie, "is for you to hold on to these, and if you see the landlord you can give them to him. That's not too much, is it?"

The woman, probably realizing that the only way we would leave was if she took the cards, relented. "I can take them, but like I said, I hardly ever see him."

"Thank you," said Millie graciously. "And please tell him when you see him that the people he is trying to evict have nowhere to go. We can't leave our home, and if we have to, we'll come back up here again."

The woman nodded, and with a painful grimace took our cards, evidently wincing at the thought of having to deal with us in the future. We walked down the steps and back to the car, followed by the security guards on their bikes. Everyone was convinced that the woman was lying, but we were in high spirits after being able to disrupt the landlord in his own home and were pleased to find a sympathetic story in the news the following week.

Still, the reaction we were hoping for never came. Over the next week I made numerous calls to the property manager and landlord but never heard back. It seemed that they were going to try and wait us out. So, with the next court date nearing, we figured that it was time to ratchet up the pressure. Michael and Millie were scheduled to be in court on a Tuesday morning, and we decided to hold a candlelight vigil that Monday evening in front of the property manager's home, hoping that our action would be fresh in their minds when we met in court.

We sent out a press release early Monday morning and received immediate interest from reporters. The story—a brother and sister being evicted from their home of seventy-three years—evoked sympathy and had all the makings of a perfect "human interest" piece. Still, from past experiences I knew that press coverage was always unpredictable. So when I heard that a number of major television networks and two daily newspapers said that they wanted to cover the event I was elated and a bit overwhelmed. As members prepared for the vigil back at the office, I headed over to Michael and Millie's apartment to oversee the reporters who wanted to show up and interview them in their homes before the vigil.

When I arrived at Michael and Millie's, I found a camera crew already there, and shepherded them in. A few minutes later, just as they were getting ready to film, two more channels showed up, then a fourth. While each reporter interviewed the siblings, the others waited impatiently in the hallway as I filled them in on the details of the case. After forty-five minutes, with all the interviews completed, Millie and I headed over to the vigil, leaving Michael to rest his infected leg upstairs in bed. As we left to catch a cab, he called out to wish us luck.

When we arrived at the vigil, we were greeted by twenty members who had gathered in front of the apartment. Millie spoke about her case to the reporters, and we ended by breaking into song. Our renditions of "If I Had a Hammer" and "De Colores" didn't exactly create a beautiful sound, but they were loud enough to gain attention from passing pedestrians. As we were singing, some of the people on the street joined in, making our group even bigger. A police car cruised by slowly, the officer peering out suspiciously at our crowd of singing citizens. I could imagine his dilemma: was public, unannounced song illegal? It certainly seemed, from the hard look on his face, that it ought to be.

Annie Mae, a senior homeowner who had become involved with PACC after signing a predatory loan, held the seventy-three flowers we were going to deliver to the property manager to symbolize the number of years the siblings had lived in their home.*

She walked up to the door of his apartment, followed by the television cameras in the cramped hallway of the building, and knocked on his door. Not surprisingly, no one answered. We placed the flowers at his doorstep, complete with a card signed by community members asking that he allow the seniors to stay.

That evening we were the lead news story on three major networks and NY1, the city's all-news network, which ran the story the next day as well. While in court the following morning, I received a call from the public advocate of New York City, Betsy Gotbaum, who had heard about the case from the coverage and wanted to know what she could do to help. Two newspaper reporters, as well, were in court covering the case.

After more than three hours of negotiations, the landlord and property manager finally agreed to grant the siblings an extension of two years. Though we had been looking for a longer term—hoping for a five-year lease—we felt satisfied with the result. They had no obligation to offer more than six months to the siblings, so there was no legal cover to hide behind. What we had made clear, however, was that a group of dedicated community members would be more than willing to take unorthodox actions and confront them at their homes, businesses, and even synagogues, bringing their "legal" problem into the plain view of their friends and family. They decided that they didn't want to take that risk.

---

* Predatory loans are high-interest and unaffordable loans granted to homeowners, often with hidden fees, that seek to strip the borrower of her equity. When individuals like Annie Mae default on such loans, the collateral (home) is seized by the lender (though in Annie Mae's case, PACC was able to save her home).

THE IMPORTANCE OF FUN

The two direct actions chronicled in this chapter, though focusing on different targets and having different demands, shared much in common. First, and not least important, they were all very much *fun*. Yes, fun—fun for the organizers and fun for the members. A good way for an organizer to judge whether he's taking his job too seriously is to pause midway through an action and see if a smile is on his face. Sure, some direct actions might be stressful and somber, but an organizer should not be taking himself so seriously that he can't enjoy the process of challenging the powerful. An organizer who is always gravely serious can be on a quick route to burnout and may turn off members in the process.

The enjoyment of direct action is equally important to members, who will be much more likely to turn out in the future if they remember having fun at an earlier direct action. It is important to remember that although motivated by lofty ideals like justice and equality, people are also more willing to be a part of a group and dedicate time to that group if they enjoy themselves in the process. As Randy Shaw writes in *The Activist's Handbook,* "Confronting an adversary on his or her own turf creates a rush of excitement often missing from political activity. Activists looking back on prior struggles tend to remember such incidents fondly, even if the tactic brought only mixed success."[5]

THE IMPORTANCE OF SURPRISE

Beyond being fun (though part of the fun) is the fact that direct actions have an air of unpredictability and spontaneity. Both direct actions described above took their targets by surprise and kept them off balance. The Department of Health didn't know what to do with a group that clogged up its lobby and refused to leave. The property manager had no idea that one day he would look out his window and find a group of people protesting, accompanied by television cameras.

In Alinsky's *Rules for Radicals,* he offers some advice about tactics just as relevant today as when he wrote about them in the 1960s. One of the rules he discusses is the need to "go outside the experience of the enemy." This will help confuse the target and can provoke damaging counterreactions on their part, fitting into Alinsky's famous formula: "Pick the target, freeze it, personalize it, and polarize it."[6] Direct action catches the powerful off guard and forces them to debate your subject on unfamiliar and embarrassing terrain.

By confronting targets, direct actions can be extremely effective —as long as they are tied into and articulate a particular demand. As Shaw writes, direct actions should be more than just fun:

> *The thrill of taking direct action, however, should not be equated with the achievement of specific goals. For example, picketing and chanting in front of your adversary's corporate headquarters may create community spirit, but if the activity is not connected to specific demands, then the action does not advance the organization's agenda . . . engaging in unfocused direct actions drains organizational and volunteer energy and creates a false sense that people are working for social change.*[7]

Successful direct actions, then, need to not only catch the target off guard but to articulate a certain end that you are trying to achieve.

THE IMPORTANCE OF ACCESSIBILITY

There is also a strong pragmatic argument for engaging in direct action: usually it's all we've got. Groups without institutional power don't have the ability to gain the attention of targets through the traditional means. The roles that poor people, undocumented immigrants, and other disenfranchised and alienated individuals can play in traditional politics are highly circumscribed, as it requires as prerequisites both extraordinary resources and political connections.

No one from the Department of Health was going to call our members and ask for their input. Landlords won't consult with their tenants or other community residents before they decide to evict people. We're locked out of institutional power, just as our targets insulate themselves from genuine community concern. Direct action can force the disinterested and hostile to wake up and pay attention, using the old-fashioned emotions of fear and embarrassment. Our adversaries like to behave as if they're in a tension-free vacuum, able to pursue whatever policy seems advantageous to their interests. Direct action brings the tension to their front door.

THE IMPORTANCE OF LEADERSHIP DEVELOPMENT

Who can forget the courageous actions of Rosa Parks, Mahatma Gandhi, and Nelson Mandela? Reading about their successful struggles for justice against such overwhelming odds, we are struck by the awesome risks they took, risks that can seem so alien to those we confront in our daily lives. But the most important lesson to be taken from such figures is usually forgotten: we fail to remember that they were also human and made their decisions not as all-knowing individuals but as people faced with specific choices. As Charles V. Willie reminds us, "By idolizing those whom we honor, we do a disservice both to them and to ourselves. . . . We fail to recognize that we could go and do likewise."[8]

A key lesson that organizers help impart is that regular people can become effective public actors, and no tactic helps impart this truth better than direct action. Through taking direct action, people learn that they have an influence that they were previously unaware of. When people engage in direct action for the first time, they learn that they can go out and, remarkably, make their voices heard. With such revelations made apparent in a concrete way, confidence develops.

But beyond the community-building that results from direct action (it's fun), the efficacy of direct action (it works), and its pragmatic rationale (it's accessible) lies another benefit, perhaps the most important in the long run: it develops. Direct action allows people—sometimes for the first time in their lives—to see themselves as "doers," as makers of history in a real way.

Leadership development, which will be covered in more detail in Chapter 4, is a critical component of community organizing. And direct actions—which members help plan and execute—are a training ground, where people get to step into unknown roles and at the end of the day assess what worked and what didn't for future events.

———

Direct action, more than any other tactic, is what makes organizing unique, set apart from other methods of social change. Sure, we'll cooperate with groups that do what we want. Sure, we'll agree to negotiate at times and hold official meetings to show that our group is "reasonable." But when push comes to shove, and targets refuse to do what we want, communities have a potent weapon in direct action. It's a way of saying to groups with power: we make our own rules here. No matter where you're at, we'll find a way to hold you accountable.

Chapter 3

A WORD OF CAUTION:
The Forgotten Photograph

> *The trouble with many of us, and with our culture as a whole, is that we don't take time to "relate," to connect formally but meaningfully with others. . . . We forget or deny that the appetite to relate is fundamental, and that the willingness to relate is nearly universal. People who have ideas and drive are on every street, in every project, every workplace and school, waiting in the wings, ready to be discovered. Someone has to reach them and recognize them. Someone has to ask them to step out, not to be consumers of props or spectators but to be players in the unfolding drama of public life. And that someone is what we call a leader or organizer.*
> —Michael Gecan[1]

As discussed in the previous chapter, direct action is the visible muscle of organizing, the brawn of protests, pickets, and chanting that most people associate with social movements. But just as with bodybuilding or running a marathon, this brawn doesn't come about organically—it must be developed through dedication and long hours of effort.

On a day-to-day level, these long hours get to the core of community organizing. Peeling off the romantic layers of the left, forgetting for the moment terms like struggle and solidarity and justice, one is left with a very important and often overlooked aspect of organizing and the making of social movements: relationship-building. Of all the tasks that an organizer engages in, by far the most hours of each day are spent building relationships with new people and deepening relationships with those one already knows. The adrenaline-inducing excitement of direct action, in fact, probably makes up less than 0.5 percent of any organizer's time.

Above my desk I have a photocopied picture from an anthology of the civil rights movement. It is a photo taken during the early 1960s in Georgia. In the photo, two African-American organizers from a civil rights group, the Student Nonviolent Coordinating Committee (SNCC), are hanging out on the porch talking to a family about the need to register to vote.

I had this certain book for years before ever paying any special attention to the photo. It is entirely unremarkable; one can feel the heat from the Southern sun, the relief of the thick shade offered by the porch, the deliciousness of a glass of cold water. It is dwarfed by the more dramatic images of sit-in students being beaten and drenched with ketchup, or King leading marchers across the Selma Bridge. There is no denying the sheer photogenic quality of the era, and progressive forces used the media with admirable skill to sway public opinion to their side. If there were a hall of fame for revolutionary images, the walls would be lined with photographs from the civil rights movement.

But the overlooked photo represents an important omission. The civil rights movement sought to alter revolutionarily the status of poor African-Americans in the South—who were one of the most institutionally powerless groups in America. What SNCC and other civil rights organizations needed to do was communicate a message of hope to these Southerners, to work to establish relationships with them and convince them that the time to agitate for change had come. Even when the organizers were from the South and familiar with the locals, they had to work to overcome the years of distrust and fear that had built up in African-Americans who had suffered from white abuse. It was a task that only community organizing, with its emphasis on grassroots education, training, and involvement, could have accomplished.

Behind revolutionary jargon lies the very ordinary and labor-intensive task of talking to people, gaining their confidence, and recruiting them to become active members of an organization. It is easy to become so enamored with activist rhetoric that one forgets how things actually end up getting better: a lot of grunt work, usually unrecognized, undertaken by unknown folks. For those with romantic illusions of nonstop action and spectacular victory upon victory, this chapter paints a more cautionary yet at the same time hopeful picture.*

RELATIONSHIP-BUILDING AND THE CREATION OF HOPE

Think for a moment about the phenomenon of team sports. A successful coach motivates players to perform at their best, and as the players become closer to each other, they construct a team culture that enables them to succeed. The players usually have a simple goal—to score more points than the other team. As the team puts in hours of practice, they learn more skills and find themselves achieving some level of mastery. As they win, their belief that they are going to continue to win grows; the team becomes confident. Organizing follows essentially the same format. Bring people together, develop relationships and trust,

---

* Perhaps it is deceiving to label the task of relationship-building as "cautionary." I do not mean to imply that it is less fun, less meaningful, or less effective in creating social change than direct action; one cannot exist without the other. I choose to use the word caution because we are popularly taught to think of social change as coming about by walking in a few marches and chanting a few slogans, quick bursts of largely spontaneous euphoria and hope. But behind every dramatic direct action lies hours of more mundane relationship-building, and "caution" is meant to convey the simple truth that the relationship-building that leads to social movements is no easy feat.

build some skills, win small victories, win bigger victories, and change some institutions in the process. Sounds good.

What, then, makes organizing such a difficult activity? One factor is the feeling of hopelessness that seems pervasive when it comes to actually making a difference in the world (not in the clichéd, give-everything-away-to-the-homeless notion, but instead the idea that people can come together and fix their own problems). Cynicism and hopelessness are not, however, instinctive sentiments. They come about because people have tried to do something, failed, and been told repeatedly that they've failed, until this failure is accepted with a simple shrug of the shoulders and a determination not to fall for such foolish aspirations in the future. It's as if any potential team that might emerge is hampered by abusive coaches set on destroying the idea that individuals working together can overcome remarkable odds. Such "coaches" are not difficult to find, and I ran into my fair share while organizing in Brooklyn.

Although to an extent this is a problem for folks of all social strata, it can be an insidious problem for low-income people who have had, at many turning points in their lives, someone reminding them that they have failed. By the time I met many of the tenants in Brooklyn, they had just suffered a string of devastating losses: a relative with a medical emergency forcing them to miss work; a boss that fired them for the missed days; a check that didn't come as a result; a landlord that didn't get that check and started an eviction process; an attorney that had tried to intimidate them in housing court. It's not difficult to see why such a person would feel hopeless and under attack from all sides. Yet I found that this initial sense of hopelessness *could* be countered, and many of the tenants who came in seemingly without hope went on to become important community leaders and in turn helped support others in need.

What is the secret to facilitating this transformation? When I speak to groups about community organizing, this question invariably comes up. This is a question that is always on an organizer's mind: there can be a general feeling that the people in the neighborhood where *we're* working, or on the issues for which *we're* fighting, or at the specific time period in which *we're* organizing make it especially difficult to organize. So I've had African-Americans tell me about how they've got to be more like the Latinos and get together, and I've had Latinos tell me that if only they followed in the footsteps of African-Americans they'd finally see some progress. In organizing, there can be a tendency to fall into the "grass is always greener" trap.

But the question does always come up: How do you get people, especially vulnerable populations like undocumented immigrants—with whom I frequently work—to become active? When people ask me this during workshops, my answer is always the same: *I* don't really do anything. I'm not being glib. When we've transformed people from intimidated spectators to active participants, it's not simply because I said something special to them during a one-on-one conversation or because I gave them some bit of legal information that made them feel more comfortable (though these things may help). It has almost always been because they eventually met other undocumented immigrants in our organization who are acting despite their legal status. Often it is not the individual organizer but community members who are able to convince others to join. In organizing, sometimes the messenger *is* the message.

In this respect, one can think of a good community organizer as behaving like Crazy Glue. As people retreat into isolating activities such as watching television, an organizer's job is to bring them out of their boxes and connect them with others who also are isolated. When an organizer can glue enough people together, they can begin the process of realizing common needs and aspirations and start to view others as friends and allies instead of enemies to distrust. They also become more powerful and can gain the confidence to confront abusive corporations, dishonest politicians, corrupt unions—indeed, any target they determine to be preventing them from achieving their goals and meeting their needs.

———————

Building relationships is not the easiest thing to write about, because it is a bit like falling in love—messy, unpredictable, hard to quantify. But the more one works as an organizer and the more people one meets, the more effective one becomes in learning how to engage people, encourage them to open up, and be able to size up whether in fact they might want to become involved (or on the other hand, whether we actually want them—I've met a few people I initially thought could be great leaders who started spouting off racist epithets. It's important to remember that organizers don't want *everyone* in the organization).

These skills are in essence people skills, and I have come to believe that almost anybody who works at them can become effective. I present myself as exhibit A in this regard, as I am normally a reserved and shy person for whom reaching out to a bunch of strangers initially seemed overwhelmingly intimidating. But I found that with experience I began to enjoy this aspect of organizing as much as any other.

And there is something of a science, which we'll dive into in this chapter, that guides an organizer's work in building relationships. If we don't have some sort of structure to recruit new people and deepen the involvement and commitment of recent recruits, then it becomes very difficult to know how effective we're being and whether we're building up toward something or just spinning our wheels.

THE BOTTOM LINE IN ORGANIZING:
Bringing New People In

There are many tactical skills that will help an organizer be effective. This book outlines many of them, from staging successful direct actions and conducting research to working with the media and encouraging people to take on leadership roles. But there is one skill that is by far the most important and without which everything else becomes meaningless. *An organizer must bring new people into the organization.*

It is easy to become so infatuated with technical organizing terminology, catchy graphics, and sexy Web sites that one forgets this bottom line. Organizers aren't in the business of simply having the coolest slogans or the most articulate talking points but identifying and bringing in previously unaffiliated people who can fight together. In part, much of the focus on other items of minimal importance, like creating beautiful flyers or building the best Web site, is a reflection on how laborious the process of organizing is. I've seen people—including myself—spend days working out the precise wording of a flyer, convinced that the dozens of hours in front of the computer will lead others to jump right in once they have the sheet of paper in their hands. But as long as we're in the office, internally debating the most effective strategy or plotting out all sorts of grand plans in our heads, we're not in the streets, where the people who will make our organization actually are to be found. So the first step in building relationships, one I would do well to remember, is to get out of the office!

DOOR KNOCKING:
The Road to Revolution

The first stage in developing relationships is also the most laborious. Door knocking is, of course, a skill like any other. One can perfect the technique of going door-to-door, learning how different approaches work better in certain communities or with certain individuals. But notwithstanding this skill, door knocking is primarily a grunt-it-out activity, demanding more relentless determination than finesse. Consequently, it is probably the weakest point for many groups doing organizing. If one does not prioritize door knocking from the beginning, it can easily be forgotten.

When people hear the words door knocking, they usually think of canvassers who come to the door asking for donations for some cause. But door knocking and canvassing are very different. Canvassers go door-to-door soliciting money, week after week after week. Generally they are canvassing for items that are far removed from the day-to-day problems experienced by the people answering the door. But a more important distinction is that canvassers aren't canvassing to identify leaders who can work together to fight for common interests but to find people who can write a check for an organization. Canvassers may help fund a movement, but they don't help build a movement. In contrast, organizers door knock first and foremost *to identify people who can become active in the actual work of the organization, which will involve not "giving" so much as "joining."* The first contact at the door is hopefully the beginning of a long relationship, not simply the collection of money.

Organizers must door knock consistently because, as Wade Rathke, who helped found the Association of Community Organizations for Reform Now (ACORN), states about the nature of an organization: "If it isn't growing, it's dying."[2] An organizer must assume that some people will become engaged but then, for a variety of reasons, lose interest and move on. Though a thoughtful leadership development component, discussed in the following chapter, will help retain individuals for the long haul, many will be faced with life's inevitable complications and drop out. That is why regular door knocking is so important for organization maintenance.

Early on in Brooklyn, I was introduced to a new term: organizer's math. This referred to the number of people one needed to talk to before finding someone who was interested in hearing what one had to say—I think it was put at one in thirty or some similarly dispiriting ratio. This was borne out in the majority of my experiences door knocking, though I found that going out with a community member to knock on doors significantly raised our success rate; people opening the door seemed more comfortable being greeted by two folks instead of a lone young white male (many, no doubt, suspected that I was somehow connected to immigration enforcement and trying to figure out their status).*

But even with this success, door knocking still reminds us that terms like "grass roots" and "organizing" do a superb job of glossing over frequently mundane and disappointing events. The bottom line is that there were many times in Brooklyn when I went out and door knocked for hours without finding anyone who was interested in what I had to say.

And yet, with all the difficulties inherent in door knocking, it remains a time-honored way of building a base for power. Although the vast majority of modern-day political leaders rely on television commercials and mass mailings, some, like the late senator from Minnesota, Paul Wellstone, focus instead on exactly this type of door-to-door organizing to build support. As Jim Hightower writes about Wellstone's philosophy in training fifteen thousand volunteers to bring their message to the doors of Minnesotans:

> The most productive thing that a campaign can do is to talk directly to people—not send mail to them, phone them or reach for them through their television set but have a real person standing in front of them at their door, really engaging them. . . . Such deep organizing not only produces victories; it also surfaces and develops a pool of skilled talent, builds a progressive grassroots infrastructure for organizing battles and—most important—nurtures future generations of leaders.[3]

---

* In addition, going door knocking with community leaders is a critical leadership development tool, as it allows members to become organizers themselves.

"Deep organizing," to use Hightower's perceptive phrase, usually begins with the simple act of going out into the neighborhood and knocking on doors.

When door knocking, the first thing to remember is that many people, for a variety of reasons, will instinctively hesitate to talk to you. One Saturday afternoon I went out to a small building that I'd noticed a week earlier. From the outside one could see a few broken windows and that the entrance, where a door must have formerly hung, was now open to all; it seemed certain that the tenants inside were living in substandard housing. I walked up the stairs and knocked on the door of the first-floor apartment. An older Latina woman opened the door.

"Hi, my name is Gabriel and I work with tenants from the Pratt Area Community Council," I said in Spanish. She looked at me blankly. "We help tenants against landlords who don't do repairs," I added, hoping this might strike a chord.

She didn't move; was she deaf? But she had heard my knock, hadn't she? "Are there any problems in this building?" I asked.

She looked up at the ceiling above me, which was shedding plaster due to obvious water damage, then cast her eyes on the floor, where the plastic tiles were coming up to reveal a dusty wooden floor.

"No, there are no problems right now," she told me. "Everything is okay in this building."

Behind her left leg peeked out a small child. She grinned at me and then went running down the hall, and I noticed she was wearing a sweater and knit cap.

"Do you have heat?" I asked.

"No, not right now. I don't know why not . . . the landlord, we haven't seen him."

"But it's freezing right now, and you've got children in the house. That's no good for them. You need to get the heat on. Do you have hot water?"

"No. I heat water on the stove," she said matter-of-factly.

"That must get expensive, all that gas you're using. That's money that the landlord owes you, 'cause he's supposed to be paying for the hot water in the building."

She found this suggestion amusing and finally broke her deadpan face with a smile. "Owes *me?* He's never around, how am I going to get him to pay me? He doesn't care."

"Well, he'll care if you take him to court. Or if he doesn't then that's fine, the City will do it. You have to heat water every day?"

"I'm not going to go to court," she replied. "My friend used to go to court all the time and nothing ever happened. It's a waste of time."

"You don't have to take him to court. Just call the number for complaints and they should send someone out. You have to heat water every day?"

"Of course, I'm not going to give cold baths. Every morning we heat up the water so we can wash."

"Here, you should call the City to complain. It's your right to have heat and hot water, and if the landlord doesn't want to give it, the City will make him pay. We're working with lots of tenants in this neighborhood whose landlords don't do repairs and don't have heat and hot water. We're having a meeting next week. If you're interested you can come along to learn what we can do."

"This number—they speak Spanish?" she asked skeptically.

"Yeah, and you can make the complaints without telling them your name. 'Cause everyone else in the building doesn't have heat or hot water, if you don't."

"Okay, that sounds good," she said, satisfied.

"Can I have your name and telephone number," I asked—looking for the most prized possession for organizers out door knocking. "So I can remind you about our meeting and send out some more information."

She gave me her contact information (victory!) and then told me I should talk to the family upstairs as well, because they had many children and were always complaining about their apartment. I gave her some information about PACC, told her I'd be calling her about the meeting, and headed upstairs to continue door knocking. The following week I called her to invite her to a meeting, and she came. She told us at the meeting that she had called the city but still didn't have heat and hot water.

"That's normal," said a PACC member named Sam, whose building had more than two hundred housing code violations on record but still didn't have hot water. "They do nothing for us. That's why we're here: to change it so that we can get what we deserve."

From being uninterested, even hostile, she was now at a community meeting expressing concern about a neighborhood problem that had once been her own private battle. It started with someone knocking on her door.

A wonderful historical example of the power of recruitment through sustained agitation is provided by a group of farmers who more than a century ago nearly organized the restructuring of the American economy. One of the most profound and inspiring movements, yet frequently underestimated and mischaracterized, was that of the Farmers' Alliance—the Populists—which involved hundreds of thousands of poor farmers, both black and white, during the late nineteenth century.★

A key propeller of the movement was the "traveling lecturers," who would canvass the South and recruit people to the gospel of cooperative trusts, economic democracy, and eventually an independent political party. These lecturers (organizers) enabled some of the most exploited and disenfranchised American citizens to mount an offensive that went to the heart of an oppressive economic system and stirred terror in the ruling class, a movement that to this day has not been equaled. Again, it all started because

---

★ The period is chronicled masterfully by historian Lawrence Goodwyn in his landmark study, *The Populist Moment,* which is essential reading for budding organizers.

people had enough nerve and passion to get out of their homes and talk to their neighbors.

ONE-ON-ONES
(aka Personal Visits or Home Visits)

The people we meet when door knocking are called "cold contacts," folks who know nothing about the organization and whom we also know very little about. But after we've spoken to them briefly, they're no longer "cold," and the next step is to follow up with them. Nothing hurts an organizer more than going out and door knocking, talking to lots of interested people and getting their contact information, and then failing to follow up. This destroys the credibility of the organizer and the organization, and organizers must always remember that without the means to do follow-up (this necessitates keeping good records) door knocking won't get one very far.

It takes more than a five-minute conversation in someone's doorway to develop a meaningful relationship between individuals and the organization, which is where one-on-ones come in. One-on-ones are just what they sound like: a chance for the organizer to sit down individually with a community member who has exhibited some leadership potential or interest and may be on the verge of becoming more involved. Whether an organization calls these visits one-on-ones, home visits, or personal visits, the idea remains the same—they are a deliberate effort on the part of the organizer to slow down to take the time needed to learn more about an individual and assess whether or not he may have the potential to become a leader in the organization.

People get involved with organizations for different reasons and have various views about what the problems are that they would like to see solved. One-on-ones are held so that organizers can better understand what a member's particular thoughts, dreams, and motivations are. They offer a chance for the organizer to listen to the concerns of people more than for the organizer to impart knowledge or make judgments. They can be used as well to agitate and prod, but one-on-ones are primarily a chance for organizers to listen—and listen carefully.

One-on-ones also acknowledge the importance of "regular" community members, who may not be accustomed to such attention regarding their interests and concerns. Just as with our community meetings, to which we invited people who are usually left out, I often held one-on-ones with people who seemed a little bewildered by my desire to know what *they* thought. One-on-ones help keep the emphasis on the people in the community and the evolution of the problems they face, so that campaigns are consistently informed and directed by the membership.

One-on-ones are very time-consuming, illustrating again the slow nature of organizing for power and social change. At first I was quite critical of one-on-ones, feeling my time would instead be better spent handing out leaflets in populated areas so that I could reach many more people. The problem was that almost no one responded after simply being handed a piece of paper. I was initially depressed and focused on the content and style of the leaflets, convinced that if I found just the right graphic or wording, I'd get better results. But then I realized that these same people are receiving papers every day with much greater promises than our organization could make—"Lose thirty pounds in one week!"; "Earn thousands of dollars from home in minutes!"—and it wasn't hard to figure out why my pamphlets went ignored.

Instead of focusing solely on handing a piece of paper to hundreds of people, organizers need to spend extended time with a few, because it is the core leaders who will then be identified who will really make or break an organizing effort. One-on-ones are an investment in time and resources, a recognition that individuals are important and that their thoughts need to be taken seriously. As with door knocking, if clear goals aren't set out periodically in terms of how many one-on-ones an organizer will aim to hold each month, it is quite easy to forget all about them in the rushed world that we inhabit. So, with door-knocking and one-on-ones, I've found that the best method is to make a plan—with numbers included—and follow it. These numbers would include items like how many doors an organizer aimed to knock on, how many new contacts they would make (name and phone number), how many one-on-ones would be held, and how many people would come to an action or a meeting. Though it can be a laborious process, there is no shortcut to building a base.

———————

After all this talk of theory, let's move from the abstract to the concrete. To build relationships and a base, we knock on doors, hold personal visits, and invite people to become active in our work. So what does this look like in the real world? Below is an example of how we moved one person into being active in our organizing work. Let's call the individual Mr. Carlson.

Tactic	Door Knocking	Personal Visit	Accountability Session	Membership Meeting
Date	Day 1	Day 6	Day 15	Day 30
Notes	Has four young children, worried about whether lead is in their home. Building is in very bad shape, with rats, roaches, leaks, etc. Told us where other parents live in the building.	Is angry about lead poisoning; sister's daughter was poisoned. Joined PACC and committed to coming to accountability session. Wants to help make sure we force NYC to take action quickly.	Attended even though it was raining very hard and there was a flash-flood advisory.	Couldn't make it to meeting, had a family emergency.

When you move into the real world, you can see how quickly things become more complicated than any tidy theory allows. We met Mr. Carlson door knocking one day, when we were speaking to people about the lead-poisoning crisis in Central Brooklyn in the context of our campaign against the Department of Health. We were door knocking to identify leaders and also to recruit for turnout for a large meeting that we were holding with representatives from the department. At the door Mr. Carlson told us that he had children and that he was concerned about the risk of them being lead-poisoned and then gave us his contact information.

A few days later, we called to set up a personal visit. Usually it goes something like, "Hi, Mr. Carlson, this is Gabriel from PACC. I stopped by a couple of days ago to talk to you about the lead-poisoning problem in the neighborhood and what we're doing to make sure the city takes care of it. When would be a good time for me to stop by and talk a bit more about the work?"

At this point, Mr. Carlson could say that he wasn't interested anymore and never to call him back. Were that to happen, he'd no longer be a contact. But when we called, he was friendly, and we set up a time to meet. At the personal visit, the organizer learned that the daughter of Mr. Carlson's sister had been lead-poisoned recently, which meant he had some personal experience with the issue. He joined the organization by paying his dues—$25 a year—and committed to coming to a large meeting we were holding with the Department of Health in two weeks. (In organizing terms, called an accountability session—see the "Organizing 101" glossary.)

Mr. Carlson is now a very hot contact: he's shown commitment by joining, he has a close relative who is personally affected by the issue, he has small children himself who could be at risk due to the poor building conditions, and he's stated that he thinks the city should take action to address the problem.

On the day of our accountability session with the Department of Health, the weather didn't cooperate. One hour before we were set to begin, the daylong drizzle developed into a downpour, and newscasters were warning about potential flash floods. Still, Mr. Carlson made the half-mile trek to the meeting, along with more than a hundred others. This, more than anything to date, demonstrated commitment. After the meeting, we called to thank him for coming and invited him to our next membership meeting so that he could meet some of our other active leaders and socialize. However, he was not able to attend due to a medical emergency. Organizers gave him a call a few days later to let him know what had transpired at the meeting and to begin to work with him and the other tenants of the building to get repairs completed.

Though it doesn't always work out so neatly, the basic format is universal: organizations build a base through talking to many people, finding those who are interested and show leadership potential, following up with them to develop a meaningful relationship, and eventually moving them to become involved in carrying out the work of the organization. In every organizer's head, then, there are many relationships that are constantly being managed—from new contacts who need to be followed up on, to more developed leaders who need some assistance in whatever is going on, to core leaders who could use some technical guidance (with preparing testimony, planning out direct actions, etc.). Part of an organizer's job is being able to juggle these many relationships and to prioritize who needs to be contacted when, so that people who might be interested in getting involved don't drop off and become forgotten.

THE MAGIC OF MEETINGS

The first action that many people will commit to is attending a community meeting. When door knocking, I would often invite people to an upcoming neighborhood meeting as well as introduce them to the organization.

To people who have spent hour after hour twiddling their thumbs through professional (and mandatory) meetings, it may seem silly to call them magical. I can understand the skepticism. I myself have little patience for meetings that are called with no real purpose or are full of self-righteous grandstanding. As an organizer there was nothing I dreaded more than the monthly meetings I had to attend to fulfill our City contract with the Housing Department. Nothing was ever accomplished, and no new information ever surfaced. It seemed that the biggest topic discussed was the weather; if we were meeting during the summer, the City official would savor our air-conditioning system, delaying her departure by stopping every few minutes to talk about this miraculous invention. To this day, I cannot remember one interesting fact ever learned at one of these meetings or a single instance where I walked out of one energized about the work I was doing. Calling meetings magical could seem to many like calling the dentist visit a pleasurable respite.

But what I found in Brooklyn was that there was nothing I enjoyed more than the meetings we held with our community members, where people came together to discuss what was going on and voice their concerns, develop an action plan, or honor people who had been active in the neighborhood. These meetings became a critical relationship-building device as my time progressed in Brooklyn.

———————

Soon after I arrived at PACC, we began holding monthly community organizing meetings at a neighborhood church. At the beginning we almost never had a set agenda, save for a few quick announcements.*

---

*This is generally not, however, an advisable practice. It is accepted by long-time organizers that good preparation is essential to productive meetings. Especially in the midst of campaigns and the development of action plans, meetings need to be well structured. But at this point, as a new organizer trying to build an initial base, I found it more helpful to keep things loose and spontaneous. As with much in organizing, being flexible is key.

The bulk of the time was spent listening to the problems of tenants facing eviction, and searching for solutions. This was partly due to our own inexperience and the lack of institutional protection: if a tenant was facing eviction in a small building, where she had no legal protection, none of us—whether professional organizers or longtime community members—had a magic answer. We were all groping around for effective tactics, a fact that helped keep the dialogue democratic and open to exploration.

For one monthly community meeting, held midway through my first year, I was especially unprepared. Artemio, my supervisor, was leaving that same week to move on to a job with organized labor, so I had been furiously absorbing as much information as possible about all of my newly inherited responsibilities. As a result, though I had been learning the finer points about how to placate city and state bureaucrats and which deadlines fell where, I had not had time to meet with PACC leaders to develop an agenda for the meeting. I was worried that we wouldn't have much to discuss. Half an hour before the start time, I scribbled down an attempt at an agenda, stuck it in my pocket, and headed over to the church where we held our evening meetings.

Walking through the front gate of the church, I was met by Marianne, a tenant who had come into the office the previous week with eviction papers. "Early too, huh?" I asked. "How is everything?"

"Things are okay," she answered. "But I don't think the landlord is going to negotiate at all." She shrugged sadly. Marianne had lived in the neighborhood for over a decade and during that time had contended with various housing code violations. Still, she wasn't eager to move, especially since rents had risen dramatically and she had three children in local schools. Not knowing what more I could do, I had invited Marianne to share her story with our members.

Once people had arrived and settled down, I introduced Marianne, and she explained how much she liked living in the neighborhood and how depressed she had become after finding eviction papers underneath her door.

Once Marianne had finished, Alberta, who had torn out her hair trying to fight against predatory lenders, offered some smooth words of counsel. "It'll be okay, girl. You're with the right people now. It'll be okay."

Others offered their support for Marianne and planned a letter writing campaign to the owner, with two members coordinating the effort. As people debated the content of the letters (should they be adversarial or polite?), I kept an eye on my wristwatch. I had invited Sandra, our first successful antieviction case, to the meeting so that she could tell Marianne about her experience, and she was running late. At a quarter to eight, as our meeting was winding down, she walked in.

"Sandra, how are you?" I asked, relieved that she had made it in time. "Everyone, this is Sandra, our first antieviction case. She started it all."

"Hi Gabriel," Sandra replied, slightly embarrassed but pleased with the hero's welcome. "Hello everyone."

We all introduced ourselves to Sandra. "I invited Sandra here tonight," I said, "even though I knew she works late, because I thought she could tell us and Marianne a little about her case. Because Sandra was in the same situation as Marianne, and she won."

People turned toward Sandra, eager to hear her story. "Well, where should I begin? I guess I'll start from the first letter." Sandra described the stress she had experienced once she found out her new landlord was trying to evict her and how eventually, through a combination of good luck, community support, and determination, she had won a two-year lease. When she finished, people broke out into applause.

"It's like an African parable I heard once," Sandra continued, not quite ready to cede the floor:

A mouse had worked for years to build a huge tent for himself and his family, only to have a lion steal it. One day, the lion left the tent to get some food, and when he came back, he heard a voice from inside. "This is my tent," the voice said. "You need to go get another one." The lion, a bit frightened by the strange voice, decided to find some of his animal friends who could help him. So he came back with a giraffe, and the two of them went up to the tent and asked for the owner of the voice to leave.

"This is my tent," a new voice responded. "You left and cannot come back and take it. Leave me alone." Finally, the lion, not knowing what to do, went to his friend the elephant and asked for his help. The lion, giraffe, and elephant all went to the tent, sure that whoever had stolen the tent from the lion would now become scared and run out.

"Get out now!" the lion yelled. "I've brought my friends Giraffe and Elephant with me, and if you don't leave immediately, we will gang up on you together."

But the voices didn't change their tune. "This is the last time we tell you, Mr. Lion. Leave us alone. This is our tent now."

The elephant, giraffe, and lion were amazed. Whoever was in that tent must be very dangerous not to be scared by the three of them. Perhaps some strange and horrible animal they'd never heard of had arrived; either way, they decided that it wasn't worth the fight, and so they left. Once they were gone, a small family of mice peeked their heads out through the tent flap, now the new owners of their old home.

"So you see," concluded Sandra, "we have a strength that we don't know. But you have to fight and you can't give up. That's why I won, 'cause I didn't give up."

As people were filing out of the room, Marianne came up to me. She had a look on her face that I hadn't seen before, a new glimmer of confidence. "I'll talk to you later this week," she told me. "I have a meeting with the attorney and will tell you what happens. I'm glad I came to this meeting. I feel much better with all these people here."★

USING MEETINGS TO RECOGNIZE LEADERS

Meetings are also an important time to recognize the efforts of members. Part of developing relationships and creating a sense of hope is convincing people that the actions they take matter—that in fact they matter more than anyone has ever told them before. It's part of what is called building a "movement culture," and by honoring community members and highlighting the work they've been doing in public, confidence grows and individuals within groups can become more committed to each other.

The unfortunate fact is that most people doing great work go unrecognized, much in the same way that though social movements depend on the efforts of many, their achievements are attributed to a few leaders. The tendency to view something like the civil rights movement solely through the prism of Martin Luther King Jr. also affects much smaller neighborhood struggles. Often at an event only one or two community members will be quoted by the press, and this type of imbalance can again create the mistaken impression that a few eloquent leaders are in

---

★ Marianne's case ended successfully. After leafleting in front of her landlord's store and sending hundreds of postcards to his home, we were able to secure an extra year for her. Just as the year was coming up she found a new apartment a few buildings down on the same street and was able to remain in the neighborhood.

charge and doing all the work. Having membership meetings to honor dedicated activists is a great way to show just how significant their work is.

While at PACC, I pushed for the creation of semiannual membership award meetings, a time to focus on the individuals who had come forward and taken action in support of threatened tenants and homeowners. PACC staff were supportive, and we decided to call this evening a celebration of "Unsung Heroes."

The idea of holding two membership award meetings a year was an important step in the push for more grassroots involvement at PACC. For years, PACC had held an annual meeting, which was a formal affair that focused more on our staff and funders, with "ordinary" people in attendance primarily as spectators. A membership award meeting, by contrast, would focus on these previous spectators and be held in a much more informal and celebratory style.

Our first award meeting happened to be scheduled toward the end of the campaign for Michael and Millie, and it made sense to recognize the folks who had been most active in that effort. We decided that since we had delivered seventy-three flowers to Michael and Millie's property manager on a chilly November evening, the least we could do was return the favor and present each activist with a rose and certificate of appreciation.

The evening of the meeting, I was nervous about the turnout. The weather was below freezing, accompanied by a nasty wind. Though we had received quite a few RSVPs, I was afraid that the inclement conditions would keep people away. But as more and more families filed in, my nerves settled down, and by the time we got started, we had gathered together our biggest meeting so far in my time at PACC—more than fifty people.

We began with an overview of PACC and a description of why we were having this meeting. Then we watched as a projector displayed the recent news coverage of Michael and Millie's case. When the lights came back on, people broke out into applause and cheers. After the clapping died down, I escorted Millie to the front, and she spoke for a few minutes about the support she had received from PACC and its members:

> My brother and I don't know where we'd be without PACC. PACC's members went up with us to Monsey, they went out to Williamsburg in the cold—and I didn't even know them before this whole thing happened. I just thank God that there was a group like PACC in the neighborhood. I think every neighborhood should have an organization like PACC.

When Millie had finished, we presented the members with roses, explaining in a few words what each person had accomplished during our campaign—from spending a few mornings out leafleting to traveling to Monsey to confront the landlord. The recipients were clearly pleased to see their work being shared with so many others, and while mingling and eating afterwards, people kept coming up to members who had been honored and congratulating them on their awards. One honoree, Julieta, beamed at me after one such congratulatory declaration: "You see, Gabriel, I'm a celebrity now. You're gonna have to start showing me some more respect."

The left is often characterized as holding an excessive number of meetings, but I've decided that this characterization is wrongheaded. It seems to me that the left suffers not due to the number of meetings but because the right people aren't being invited.

Criticizing meetings as a phenomenon is nonsense. What are schools but places to meet and discuss? Church is a series of weekly meetings that go on indefinitely. Meetings help provide the space people need to connect with others and share ideas. In an era when people "meet" six hours a day with a mechanical box that refuses to listen, groups of people coming together play a crucial humanizing function. But if meetings are important, this is especially the case for people who normally aren't invited. In a world where the people at our community gatherings are normally called to meetings only to be chastised by bosses or questioned by caseworkers, PACC's meetings were a new experience altogether.

Meetings, in this sense, are for community organizers a series of small building blocks toward democracy, allowing others to participate, argue, encourage, and relate. There is a small group of people out there, confident and talkative, whom we hear from far too often.*

And there is a large group of people conditioned to remain silent, whom we need to hear from much more often than we do. These are the people who make meetings magical.

THE TWO TRADITIONS

One of the most effective organizers in the civil rights movement was Bob Moses, who "has written that the Civil Rights Movement can be thought of as having two distinct traditions":

> There was what he labels the community-mobilizing tradition, focused on large-scale, relatively short-term projects. This is the tradition of Birmingham, Selma, the March on Washington, the tradition best symbolized by the work of Martin Luther King. This is the movement of popular memory. . . . [But there is

---

* This is the real failure, I believe, of the left: it meets frequently with like-minded and equally confident professionals—forgetting that the real source of change is not in their community but out there, in the street, waiting to be invited. The left needs to learn that if it wants to become relevant, it has to get its hands dirty and engage real people with real problems.

> *another] tradition of Black activism, one of community*
> *organizing, a tradition with a different sense of what*
> *freedom means and therefore a greater emphasis on the*
> *long-term development of leadership in ordinary men*
> *and women.*[4]

The two traditions actually complement each other: the large-scale mobilizations are often made possible only by the community organizing that builds social networks that allow for information to be spread. But the unglamorous work of organizing—this long-term process of building relationships and developing leaders—gets written out of history, just as I overlooked for years the photograph of SNCC organizers in the anthology. As organizers, our work reminds us of the essential ingredients that fuel every social movement: the difficult but rewarding tasks of bringing new people into organizations and assisting their development into leaders.

Chapter 4

THE WISDOM OF ELLA BAKER:
Strong People Don't Need Strong Leaders

If you go to the city of Washington . . . you will find that almost all of them claim, in glowing terms, that they have risen from the ranks to places of eminence and distinction. I am very glad I cannot make that claim for myself. I would be ashamed to admit that I had risen from the ranks. When I rise it will be with the ranks, and not from the ranks.
—Eugene Debs[1]

The innumerable programs supporting individual leaders constitute a mini-industry. Most of these programs are geared toward developing skills of professionals—leaders who are paid to work in their chosen fields. For the most part, they ignore the potential of lesser leaders, leaders without formal education, leaders who are poor, leaders who are immigrants or of color, and leaders whose mission requires them to be accountable to a larger community or to build organizations in which leadership is renewed.
—Rinku Sen[2]

My theory is strong people don't need strong leaders.
—Ella Baker[3]

One morning I found an envelope in my mailbox at the office. It was addressed to Marianne's landlord from the previous chapter, and attached to the envelope was a message asking me to deliver the letter directly to him. I opened it up, curious.

> *Dear Landlord,*
> *It be kind of you to let Marianne stay in her home. She in her late 30s, pretty soon she won't be able to move to another place. Her three childs need be grown up before move. If you don't it might be protest. I and a few more landlords. Between you and her work it out don't go to court. Rats in her apartment. It should not be, take care of it please.*
>
> *—Annie M. Dawson*

Annie Mae Dawson was a senior homeowner from Bedford-Stuyvesant and had originally become involved in our work after being victimized by a predatory lender. Her life, one could tell, had been hard, with many unfortunate twists and turns—and as she aged, her mental faculties had been gradually diminishing. In our meetings she normally remained quiet, sometimes more excited about the prospect of food than anything else. But when she heard the story of Marianne, something struck a nerve. During our two-week letter-writing drive aimed at Marianne's landlord, Annie Mae had taken it upon herself to send this to me so that I could deliver it.

Annie Mae had grown up in the South and after moving to Brooklyn had survived the death of her husband and then gone on to be nearly stripped of her home by loan sharks. She was about as poor and formally powerless as one can get. And yet here she was, writing a letter in broken English, purchasing a stamp, and licking an envelope in support of someone she had just met.

This heartfelt gem of a letter represented the first step into activism for Annie Mae. Weeks later, she became an active member in our newest antieviction campaign, leafleting in front of a landlord's house and talking to people about the evictions of Michael and Millie. Reaching the later years of her life, this community member was receiving the support she needed to come into her own as a leader. Though she had very real limitations on what she could accomplish, our group was helping to encourage and realize her leadership potential.

But Where Is Her Husband?

"It doesn't matter if he tries to intimidate us; we're together and we're not going anywhere," explained PACC member Julieta to the television reporter in Spanish, who was doing a story on the housing conditions of immigrant families. "We've been fighting for a long time now."

When I was speaking to the reporter later on that day, he mentioned her determination. "She is quite a character, huh?—wouldn't want to mess with her," he said, in awe of this Costa Rican woman who lived in her dilapidated apartment building in Bedford-Stuyvesant.

"Yeah, she has been a real leader in the neighborhood," I replied. "She's worked both with her own building and also helping other people in their fights."

"So strange though, I mean, where is her husband?" the reporter asked. "What is he doing about the situation?"

"Her husband has been pretty sick for awhile, with lots of health problems," I answered. "Julieta likes to shield him from the landlord, who would only stress him out." I could tell my answer didn't quite satisfy the reporter.

"Well, whatever . . . like I said, I wouldn't want to mess with her."

COMMUNITY ORGANIZING AND LEADERSHIP DEVELOPMENT:
Rejecting Conventional Wisdom

Leadership development is a third core component of community organizing, along with direct action and relationship-building. But before we jump into the topic of leadership development, we have to examine a central question: what makes a good leader?

Our society has a particular view of leadership, often unstated. Leaders are male; they speak English; they are, more often than not, white. They wear suits; they are charismatic; they shout orders and are obeyed. They give lengthy speeches; demand attention; speak "for" and "on behalf" of others. As even Martin Luther King Jr. said, characterizing this top-down leadership approach, "Leadership never ascends from the pew to the pulpit . . . but from the pulpit to the pew."[4]

The reporter interviewing Julieta held this conventional view of leadership, and his mental model made it difficult for him to label her a leader. But though we are fed very different images of leadership by the mass media and popular culture in general, there are countless leaders like Julieta and Annie Mae in every community, breaking all our inherited notions of leadership. As Linda Stout, a low-income woman who went on to build a successful community organizing group, writes in her book *Bridging the Class Divide,* "Redefining leadership is really a survival issue for people of color, women, and low-income communities. Traditional leadership has historically excluded us for the most part."[5]

Notions of leadership for organizers can revolve around an entirely different set of criteria from the inherited wisdom described above. Instead of leading through being unusually loud, leaders can instead work quietly to develop other leaders and provide moral support. Being a charismatic public speaker may be a nice characteristic to possess, but without being held accountable to a group, such "leaders" usually wander far from the community's concerns and become more interested in their individual aggrandizement. Good looks and perfect English may be necessary attributes for rock stars or political candidates, but valuable community leaders come in all shapes and sizes and are frequently immigrants from other countries who may not speak a word of English.

As Rinku Sen stated in one of the quotations that opened this chapter, our country has a very strong support system out there for leadership development that people can plug into—if they are lucky enough to be highly educated and wealthy. Business executives can participate in leadership summits and political wannabes can attend sessions where they are groomed by lobbyists and elite strategists. Images of eagles soaring over forests and athletes scaling treacherous mountains are hung on office walls to remind the well-to-do of their immense potential.

But as in all societies that suffer from extreme inequality, a small group of privileged individuals receive far more assistance than needed, while millions of people are ignored—or worse—actively worn down and disparaged. Not surprisingly, the interests of the powerful are well represented, and the interests of the rest are placed aside as irrelevant or marginal. Most damaging of all, those among the so-called "irrelevant" and "marginal" may begin to believe the messages they are sent and give up hope.

As community organizers and small "d" democrats, we must remember that an entire army of people is out there *right now,* being directly affected by problems, with the potential to become leaders. Perhaps because they are immigrants, or poor, or speak limited English, or for a whole host of other reasons, they have been told by our society—directly and indirectly—that they are not capable of becoming leaders. But like many other claims of the dominant ideology in our society, this one is wrong. Latent leaders are everywhere, and good organizers recognize this fact and refuse to accept the common thinking that only a talented (and usually privileged) few have the ability to lead.

This chapter explores the theory and practice of leadership

development within community organizing, with a special focus on the need to discard much of the inherited wisdom on leadership in favor of a more democratic approach. In organizing, leadership development may be the most important skill of all; the term itself refers to the practice of working with community members to develop the confidence and skills needed to take action and play a leadership role within the organization and the community. As with relationship-building, leadership development occurs largely behind the scenes and is time-consuming and difficult to describe or quantify. Broadly put, leadership development for community organizers is the practice of and priority placed on allowing people directly affected by the issues to emerge as active participants in the struggle and aiding this development.

I have broken the rest of this chapter down into three sections. The first takes a look at one of the most original and profound thinkers on the subject, the civil rights organizer Ella Baker. Her ideas on leadership development and the critical role it plays within successful social movements provide a stimulating backdrop for a discussion on the theory behind the belief that, as she put it, "People have to be made to understand that they cannot look for salvation anywhere but to themselves."[6]

The second section of the chapter discusses the role of political education in leadership development, focusing on the popular education model championed most famously by Paulo Freire. In groups doing organizing, one aspect of leadership development that frequently gets overlooked, and that I believe to be critical to the long-term success of organizing efforts, is the continual role that political education must play. The second section examines political education in detail—from a theoretical point of view and also with real examples from my experiences in Brooklyn.

The third section chronicles the emergence of a few key

leaders in Brooklyn. After approaching the subject of leadership development through a relatively clean conceptual lens, the chapter ends by looking at leadership development as it actually occurred while organizing on the ground in New York City. I hope that these quick profiles will allow the ideas and lessons to become a bit more concrete and—paradoxically—a bit less tidy. For it must be remembered that leadership development—as with most organizing concepts—appears unrealistically clear on paper, becoming more complicated when translated into the real world. By looking at real people and their emergence as leaders, we shall see that leadership development is not a "thing" given to others but an ongoing process whereby people can slowly begin to see themselves in a different light and better understand the world around them and how they might go about changing it.

TWO CRITICAL IDEAS OF CIVIL RIGHTS ORGANIZER ELLA BAKER

Although the civil rights movement was a mass movement fighting for the democratic rights of African-Americans, within the movement itself certain decidedly undemocratic trends and beliefs existed. Foremost among them were the general convictions that men were uniquely positioned to lead and that the success of the movement depended on the actions of a few extraordinary leaders.

Such traditional notions of leadership were profoundly and repeatedly challenged by a black female organizer named Ella Baker. Throughout her life, Baker's leadership-development beliefs and the model of social change that they implied led her to clash frequently with venerable organizations such as the National Association for the Advancement of Colored People (NAACP) and even with the most famous civil rights leader of them all, Martin Luther King Jr.

Baker was a lifelong activist and organizer. During the 1930s she helped create the Young Negroes' Cooperative League, where she designed consumer cooperatives to promote group buying, enabling poor blacks to pool their limited resources to see higher values from their purchases. This experience led her to work for the Works Progress Administration (WPA) until the late 1930s, when she became a field organizer for the NAACP, traveling throughout the South seeking to establish local branches.

Crisscrossing the country helped Baker develop her philosophy on social change based on the decentralized, local empowerment of communities and citizens. The emphasis on decentralized and local power sprang from her feelings on the need for self-reliance among communities. As she said in an interview, "My basic sense of it has always been to get people to understand that in the long run, they themselves are the only protection they have against violence or injustice."[7]

After leaving the NAACP in 1946, fed up with their practice, as she saw it, of using local branches primarily to collect dues from members instead of developing local bases of power, she went on to join the staff of the New York Urban League and the New York Cancer Society. She still worked frequently with the NAACP, however, and in 1955 the mayor of New York City called on her to work for the Commission on School Integration. Soon thereafter, when the Montgomery Bus Boycott was initiated, it was again largely due to the efforts of Baker that another organization, In Friendship, was formed to support the efforts in Montgomery financially.

After the successful termination of the Montgomery Bus Boycott, the Southern Christian Leadership Council (SCLC) was created to further the struggle, again primarily as a result of pressure from Baker. She acted as the principal organizer for the group, holding it together during its first years, but became alienated by its lack of focus on grassroots work, coupled with the hesitancy of the members to carry out suggestions from a woman. In 1960 she resigned from the organization. Just a few months later she would play a key role in the founding of the Student Nonviolent Coordinating Committee (SNCC).

SNCC grew out of the student sit-in demonstrations protesting the segregation of restaurants and stores in the South. When word spread that a mass civil disobedience movement was underfoot and being led by students not directly affiliated with the established civil rights organizations, there was a feeling among some adult leaders that the students should take their place as a group under the direction of their more knowledgeable elders. Baker, fearing that the energy and outside-the-box thinking of the students could be sapped by the SCLC, stressed that the students needed the space and autonomy to chart their own course—even if this meant that they would make mistakes on occasion.

As Barbara Ransby writes in her wonderful biography, *Ella Baker and the Black Freedom Movement:*

> *Baker insisted that a movement was a web of social relationships. Charismatic leaders could rally an anonymous mass of followers to turn out for a single event or series of events; millions could watch television coverage of heroic actions by a brave few or speeches by mesmerizing orators; but that was mobilization, not organization. In order to be effective organizers in a particular community, Baker argued, activists had to form relationships, build trust, and engage in a democratic process of decision making together with community members. The goal was to politicize the community and empower ordinary people. This was Baker's model, and in 1961 it became SNCC's model.[8]*

With the founding of SNCC, Baker became one of several adult advisers (including the radical historian Howard Zinn), and her influence shaped SNCC's reliance on the need to develop local leadership, build strong relationships with the communities, and engage in militant direct action. Though Baker passed away in 1986, her profound contributions to the topic of leadership development remain, and I look at two ideas that are especially illuminating for community organizers.

Idea Number 1: There Is a Crucial Difference between "Movement-Centered" Leaders and "Leader-Centered" Movements

Ella Baker's greatest contribution to the philosophy of movement building was her distinction between "movement-centered" leaders and "leader-centered" movements. This distinction grew out of her recognition of the tendency among some to place all their faith in a certain leader whom they could rely upon for protection and strength.

Instead, she found that the most effective leaders were those who came out of the community and were representatives of movements. These leaders did not lead so much as facilitate, encourage, and empower. Movements that revolved around charismatic leaders, on the other hand, forgot that the most important aspect of enacting change was from the "bottom up," where the tedious and often thankless task of organizing for local empowerment occurred. She laid out this philosophy in an interview she gave in the 1970s:

> In government service and political life I have always felt it was a handicap for oppressed peoples to depend so largely upon a leader, because unfortunately in our culture, the charismatic leader usually becomes a leader because he has found a spot in the public limelight. It usually means he has been touted through the public media, which means that the media made him, and the media may undo him. There is also the danger in our culture that, because a person is called upon to give

public statements and is acclaimed by the establishment,
such a person gets to the point of believing that he is the
movement. Such people get so involved with playing the
game of being important that they exhaust themselves
and their time, and they don't do the work of actually
organizing people.[9]

This movement-centered leader approach depended upon the development of many local leaders, who in turn worked to develop even more leaders. If local leaders where relying on the presence and guidance of national figures, then when an organization or its national leaders pulled out, it would take with it any progress that had been made. To make matters worse, during the civil rights movement, if an organization departed a community without creating an indigenous base, the protection that the organization's presence had provided departed as well. Local people who had openly voiced their disapproval would be vulnerable to reprisals from whites long after the television crews had headed home. Baker therefore felt it essential to build a local base, and doing this required identifying natural leaders in the area who could do the work and who understood the community.

Community organizers can learn a lot from Baker's differentiation between movement-centered leaders and leader-centered movements. Leader-centered movements can collapse when the leader leaves, or sells out, or gives up. Members of leader-centered movements get their direction from the leader and become accustomed to doing what the leader says is the right thing to do without reflection or debate. Such movements become inseparable from the leaders, and the leaders of such movements frequently begin to see themselves as the movement. But if a few leaders are directing the movement, then it's not really a movement—or at least it's not a democratic movement. It's also not as strong as it may appear, being much more vulnerable and susceptible to failure because it depends upon the judgment and determination of only a select few, who can easily be led astray. In an address to workers, the famous labor leader Eugene V. Debs explains this weakness:

> *Too long have the workers of the world waited for some*
> *Moses to lead them out of bondage. He has not come;*
> *he never will come. I would not lead you out if I could;*
> *for if you could be led out, you could be led back again.*
> *I would have you make up your minds that there is*
> *nothing that you cannot do for yourselves.*[10]

Movements that renew leadership, strive to develop it evenly among its members, and hold and act upon democratic values will move in a direction decided upon collectively and be able to examine new issues as they arise without having to filter all of their information through one or two designated spokespeople.

Movement-centered leaders emerge from the group as the group develops and are held accountable by the group. These leaders are also more numerous; when the task at hand requires a certain skill, the members of the movement with that skill step forward—and the label of leader becomes much more fluid and flexible. Groups with movement-centered leaders are democratic and understand that their strength comes from their collective wisdom and action, and such a group does not unravel when one person is removed. Movement-centered leaders believe that others also have the potential to lead and understand that the success of the movement depends upon this transformation of consciousness. This understanding brings us to another related idea of Baker's.

Idea Number 2: "Strong People Don't Need Strong Leaders"

Baker believed that when people became accustomed to depending upon strong leaders for guidance, it signified that they were themselves dangerously weak. For Baker, "strong people" are to be created by the movement, and there is no prerequisite to who has the potential to become strong. Indeed, the extent of the success of a movement can be judged by how many people held an image of themselves as weak prior to their involvement and then learned their true strength through collective action.

It may seem odd to talk about the importance of leadership development by defining it as unnecessary, as Ella Baker appears to do in her statement. But what Baker is trying to stress is not that "leaders" are bad but that we need to radically rethink what characteristics make a good leader and *dramatically expand our notion of who is eligible to lead.*

When organizers dramatically expand the notion of who among the group is eligible to lead, they also become skeptical about the idea of "born" leaders. This is because the more one becomes comfortable with the concept of born leaders, the more likely one is to become comfortable with its corollary: crowded between the few "born leaders" are the rest, "born followers," who naturally follow orders and are incapable of exhibiting or developing leadership qualities. Organizers need to remember that most people who haven't yet been identified as leaders by society have simply been given neither the tools nor the opportunity to lead. An organizer's primary goal is to bring this latent potential out, to help humans more fully develop who have seen their personal growth stunted by a dysfunctional system.

Many may initially be skeptical of this dramatically more democratic notion of leadership. As Linda Stout writes:

> I suppose from a traditional perspective on power and leadership, that might look like too many leaders. But our experience at PPP [the Piedmont Peace Project, an organization founded by Stout] has shown us that the more leaders we have, the more we share leadership, and the more new people we have taking on leadership

> roles, the stronger and more powerful we become. I
> think of leadership as an expanding circle. The more
> the circle enlarges to include, the bigger and more pow-
> erful it grows, and the stronger the organization
> becomes.[11]

This emphasis on working to see the leadership potential in everyone does not mean, of course, that organizers should ignore obvious talents that various members might have. If some members are great public speakers, then it makes sense to have them do more public speaking. But for organizers, this emphasis on broad development means that we must also look at other members who are initially nervous about public speaking and do not instinctively jump into every conversation, seeing them as having the potential to blossom in the future. It means that we need always to be looking to develop new skills in people and not write off those who do not seem overwhelmingly talented from the beginning.

One way to think of what organizers do in leadership development is to conceptualize them as farmers who create and maintain a fertile soil from which members can regularly sprout into leaders. This means that much of the relationship- and community-building described in the previous chapter is essential to paving the way for leadership development. It also means, in practical terms, that organizers must have activities that people can plug into at all levels, from the simple (letter writing, making phone calls) to the more complicated (door knocking, chairing meetings, participating in campaign development, planning direct actions). When there are various activities that people can become involved in, one will be surprised just how many "leaders" are out there in the neighborhood. When one has a movement of many leaders who share power and are accountable to each other, then the dichotomy of leaders and followers can slowly erode, until the group is, in Ella Baker's words, full of "strong people."

There is a wonderful story that illustrates the hidden leadership potential that can lurk inside even the most unlikely of individuals. The "forgotten photograph" from the previous chapter captured two students who were working in the South with SNCC, which a few years later conducted Freedom Summer, an ambitious project during the summer of 1964 in the state of Mississippi. More than a thousand volunteers, primarily white students from prestigious Northern universities, traveled south to work with indigenous leaders in a campaign to register black voters and participate in other community-building activities.

This extraordinary project was studied by Doug McAdam, a sociologist from Stanford University, who wanted to discover the effects, if any, of that experiment on its participants. In his book *Freedom Summer,* McAdam followed the lives of the students after they completed the project and returned home. As one would expect, many of the students were rather remarkable (they were, after all, venturing into situations where their very lives were in jeopardy). Some, however, were less obviously gifted. One example of the latter was a nondescript student from the University of California at Berkeley. In the recollections of various people who worked with this individual, he was largely unimpressive. One woman, a civil rights activist who interviewed the individual to determine whether he ought to be recommended for participation in Freedom Summer, made the following observation:

> *Generally what I have to say about him is this: not a very creative guy altho [sic] he accepts responsibility and carries it through if you explain to him exactly what needs to be done. . . . Can't decide if I were picking people if I would choose him . . . probably he would be one of those "average" people who I'd want to see the results of . . . before making a judgment.*[12]

Others in McAdam's study echoed the above assessment. Why, many people wondered, had this individual even decided to go to Mississippi in the first place? Traveling to the South in 1964 with an explicitly antiracist agenda was a very risky proposition. If naïve students had hoped simply for some fun and adventure, ten days into the program they had been dealt a reality check: three participants, James Chaney, Andrew Goodman, and Michael Schwerner, disappeared, having been beaten to death by Mississippi segregationists opposed to the project. This, then, was not a place one would expect "average" youth to flock to, yet the individual described above managed to stick it out through the summer, though no one seemed overly impressed with his abilities.

In his book, McAdam followed the students as they returned to school the following year. Safely back in the confines of academia, a protest broke out at the University of Berkeley over the administration's refusal to allow students to staff tables and hand out political literature on campus property. Out of this campaign, the Free Speech Movement was born on the campus of Berkeley, and throughout the movement an eloquent student leader galvanized thousands, contending that:

> There is a time when the operation of the machine becomes so odious, makes you so sick at heart, that you can't take part; and you've got to put your bodies upon the gears and upon the wheels, upon the levers, upon all the apparatus and you've got to make it stop.[13]

The speaker, forever associated with the Free Speech Movement, was Mario Savio, the same student who was characterized as "average" and "not very creative" just a year earlier when he was hoping to get the chance to head to Mississippi. This quiet and unassuming student had traveled to the South and returned to Berkeley a different person, helping to lead a movement that garnered the entire nation's attention.

LEADERSHIP DEVELOPMENT
AND POLITICAL EDUCATION

One of the most critical aspects of leadership development is the engagement of members in political education. Political education, as Robert Fisher writes in *Let the People Decide,* should:

> (R)eveal the roots of people's problems in the workings of the economic and political system. . . . The role of political education, which is an analysis that grows out of people's political experience, is to broaden people's perspectives and to give them more information on which they can make more reasoned assessments of the conditions, problems, and alternative solutions they face.[14]

This pedagogical philosophy, frequently called popular education (here I use the terms popular and political education interchangeably), reached a broad audience through the writings of an educator by the name of Paulo Freire—most notably in his book *Pedagogy of the Oppressed.* In this text, an essential manual for organizers, the Brazilian Freire critiqued the repressive nature of hierarchical schooling, which exemplified what he called the "banking" concept of education:

> In the banking concept of education, knowledge is a gift bestowed by those who consider themselves knowledgeable upon those they consider to know nothing. . . . Education thus becomes an act of depositing, in which the students are the depositories and the teacher is the depositor. . . . The more students work at storing the deposits entrusted to them, the less they develop the critical consciousness which would result from their intervention in the world as transformers of that world.[15]

In his writing Freire rebels against this traditional notion of education in favor of an approach he calls "problem-posing":

> *In problem-posing education, people develop their power to perceive critically the way they exist in the world with which and in which they find themselves; they come to see the world not as a static reality, but as a reality in process, in transformation. . . . The students—no longer docile listeners—are now critical co-investigators in dialogue with the teacher.*[16]

This philosophy of education, where people's life experiences are not irrelevant to the curriculum but, indeed, central to it, and where the hierarchy between teacher and student is minimized so that people can learn together, is the pedagogical model most organizers adhere to in engaging their members in political education. This popular-education model insists that learning is a collective activity; a discussion, not a lecture. It also acknowledges that the solutions to community problems actually lie within the people being affected. There may be analytical tools that organizers can share to better help leaders think through issues, and there are many opportunities for organizers to insert their thoughts into a debate, but the heart of the political education must come out of people's own experiences.

Insisting on the importance of political education is insisting that community leaders are valuable enough to merit substantial investment. Most of the members I worked with in Brooklyn had been subjected to a dysfunctional and uninspiring educational experience, and organizing presented a wonderful chance to engage them on issues critical to them. Instead of the dread with which people remembered being forced to shut up and pay attention to someone else's lesson plan, people were animated by the opportunity to debate ideas collectively and be exposed to new ideas.

To keep things fresh, political education should include all sorts of activities. In Brooklyn we usually set aside a part of each monthly community meeting to engage people in a discussion around a problem that affected them and encouraged members to come up with and debate their own solutions. In addition, we held regular leadership development training sessions (on our own and in partnership with such groups as the New York City Organizing Support Center and the Center for Third World Organizing), which covered aspects of the work that members were engaged in, from writing press releases to doing outreach and holding direct actions. To keep things from getting dull, we also planned various hands-on activities such as arranging for our members to tour the Lower East Side Tenement Museum, where people could see firsthand the living conditions immigrant tenants faced at the turn of the twentieth century. These various activities helped keep people engaged in the work and led them to have new understandings about themselves and the world in which they were living.

BARRIERS TO CONDUCTING POLITICAL EDUCATION

There are two key reasons why organizations might not engage enough in political education. The first obstacle—as is frequently the case in the busy world of organizers—is logistical. There are always so many other tasks that need to be completed that taking time out to focus on political education may seem a luxury that one cannot afford. Many organizations, therefore, focus entirely on recruiting members, engaging in direct actions, even running campaigns, without developing a system that regularly engages their members in political education so that they can better understand and analyze the forces that shape their lives and can play significant roles in determining the direction that an organization takes.

In Brooklyn I found that organizing without focusing on a political-education component ended up feeling superficial and manipulative. Many members first came to PACC because of the individual problems they were experiencing with their landlords. I would work with them to fight their landlords, and if we won, they then felt gratitude and appreciated the help. I could count on them to come out for direct actions and didn't necessarily need to engage them on exactly what the issue was or in a dialogue of what some of the core problems might be. They sensed that something was wrong, and when I called, they would come.

But is this organizing or manipulation? Without engaging members collectively on tough issues, I was instead deciding the issues and then enlisting them. It looked like organizing, for sure, when we had thirty people protesting, but it didn't feel like organizing, because I had failed to take the time to allow members the chance to determine the course of action. Because there was no commitment to ongoing political development, people were still relying on me, in Ella Baker's phrase, as "a strong leader." By engaging members in political education, organizations can help minimize the extent to which professional organizers direct everything and use their base only when they feel it to be appropriate.

The answer to the problem of being so busy that a political-education component gets left out is simple: prioritize political education. An organizer must set aside time to work on political education and leadership development, time that is clearly apart from day-to-day crisis management and any other normal responsibilities. Organizations that value political education must be deliberate in designing programs to engage their members. The magic answer, again, is to develop a plan with clear goals and follow through with it. This is the only way organizations that are stressed for time (as all community organizing groups are) can hope to remain on track with political education even in the midst of daily responsibilities.

The second reason that organizations fail to engage in political education is more fundamental, having its origins in differences of ideological orientation among groups doing the organizing. Many organizations pride themselves on being "nonideological," influenced primarily by Saul Alinsky, who wrote that organizers have "no need for the security of an ideology or a panacea," and that they must remain politically relative and avoid becoming trapped in dogmas.[17]

Many organizers—and I count myself among them—who see this pragmatic philosophy as having serious shortcomings feel the best evidence comes from the experiences of Alinsky himself. Alinsky's first and most successful organizing experiment occurred in the "Back of the Yards" neighborhood of Chicago (the same neighborhood documented in Upton Sinclair's *The Jungle*), where he organized a neighborhood council in the 1930s to build power among dispossessed white ethnic groups. This "organization of organizations" was able to win numerous and substantial victories on issues that affected the community—what could be called bread-and-butter fights.

Though the neighborhood and the council he organized were able to win immediate and impressive victories, they also displayed some racist tendencies, which were never fully challenged by Alinsky because he was afraid (probably rightly so) that confronting the issue of race would cause the organization to implode. However, as the base became stronger, the organization evolved into a more overtly reactionary and racist group that by the 1960s was actively organizing to keep blacks out of the neighborhood. A strong organization had been created, but it turned its sights—in part due to its rudderless pragmatic orientation—away from issues of social justice. The organizers failed to engage their members in a political education that would confront them on their own racism.[18]

Pragmatism can help organizations avoid becoming ideologically rigid and may make it easier at times to build power, but neither of these should be the ultimate goal; the ultimate goal is to create a more democratic world, which will occur only through developing progressive members and activists. This means, as Rinku Sen writes, that we must discard the notion of remaining nonideological:

> [T]he notion of the non-ideological organization has been increasingly challenged as the New Right gains power and success. That notion has led many organizations to avoid ideologically difficult issues and to suppress that kind of discussion in their organizations. Activists are beginning to recognize that the non-ideological organization doesn't exist. All individuals and organizations operate from an ideology; an ideology is simply a world-view, and everyone has one, whether stated or implicit.[19]

Only by insisting that political education is important and helping to push groups to think through difficult topics such as race, sexual orientation, gender, and class can organizers hope to build democracy in the long run. Immediate issues that provide real benefits for members are critical, but we also must take the time to help people look deeper into the systematic problems of society and not be afraid to challenge the prejudices that members—and organizers—hold.

CHALLENGING HOMOPHOBIA IN BROOKLYN

Make the Road by Walking is best known in New York City for its aggressive workplace organizing, taking on many fights against abusive sweatshop owners in the industrial areas of East Williamsburg and Bushwick. The vast majority of its members are Latino immigrants, many from rural areas, who have traveled thousands of miles north in the search for work, only to deal with bosses who pay well below the minimum wage or refuse at times to pay back wages at all.

David Perez became the office manager at Make the Road after being introduced to its two codirectors by a local priest. Perez, an openly gay man at the time, was born and raised in

Bushwick and had dropped out of nearby Bushwick High School at the age of fourteen after being harassed and assaulted by students because of his homosexuality. Bushwick, a poor and working-class neighborhood, was not gay-friendly—to say the least—and Perez spent six years addicted to crack and heroin to cope, finally becoming sober at the age of twenty. As Perez told one paper, "Drugs were my body armor. They enabled me to walk down the street or take the train without fearing for my life."

While working as the office manager, Perez started a volunteer organizing effort called Gays and Lesbians of Bushwick Empowered (GLOBE). Knowing how difficult it could be for queers in Bushwick, Perez's mission was both to create a safe space for lesbian, gay, bisexual, and transsexual (LGBT) people and to conduct antibias training to begin challenging homophobia in the neighborhood—and within the walls of Make the Road as well.

Perez began taking hormones in 2002 as he transitioned into a female, Dee. While men waited in the offices to speak to an organizer or lawyer, some would make homophobic comments under their breath to each other, directed at Perez. Then antigay graffiti started showing up in the bathroom, obviously targeting Perez.

Without an overtly progressive political orientation, at this point Make the Road might have overlooked the comments and graffiti. Many of their potential members might very well have been homophobic—the office was located in the same neighborhood that had forced Perez to drop out, after all. But the issue that brought most people in was one of economic justice. Confronting workers about their antigay remarks might have led some to leave.

"But we wanted our organization to be a safe place," explained cofounder Andrew Friedman. "We made this decision on our own; it wasn't made democratically." To challenge the men who had been overheard making antigay remarks, Make the Road organized a meeting with the men, the board of directors, Perez, and members of GLOBE.

"It was just one of those awesome meetings," recalled Friedman. "These guys [the workers] didn't even really know what they were doing, how much pain they were causing with their remarks." GLOBE members spoke about how they had been discriminated against and shared their stories of overcoming adversity. The men apologized for their comments, and a notice was posted in the bathroom, signed by the board of directors, stating that Make the Road was an organization that welcomed everyone and that anyone promoting a homophobic message would be kicked out of the group. In addition, as a part of raising consciousness and changing behavior, GLOBE now conducts homophobia workshops for all members of Make the Road as well as at local high schools (including Bushwick High, which Perez had been chased out of as a teenager).

With the continual political education, many of Make the Road's members have become more accepting, though there is always more work to be done. "Homophobia still exists, of course," said Friedman. "But we're building a critical mass of people who won't accept it. Some people might not like it [the challenge against homophobia] and are still uncomfortable. But they have to deal with it if they're going to be a member." By challenging its own members on their homophobia, Make the Road was creating a safe space for LGBT people in Bushwick and confronting homophobia head-on. For many people who walk through Make the Road's doors, it should be remembered, this is the only place where they're going to hear this message.

LEADERSHIP DEVELOPMENT IN BROOKLYN:
Three Stories

Leadership development, like many other facets of organizing, can be reduced to a relatively simple phenomenon. Leaders develop when they are provided the support, inspiration, and guidance needed to evolve into people who can achieve more than they previously believed possible. Stated most concisely, leadership development occurs when individuals take on new roles and behave in ways previously unimagined, with a result that they begin to hold a new notion of themselves and of their ability to create change in the world.

The following section documents the emergence of three very different individuals as they became leaders in Brooklyn: Enida, Enrique, and Jedidah. Their stories are told to make the practice of leadership development more concrete and to look at some of the methods organizers can use in real life to develop leaders.

Enida and Our First Membership Meeting

One evening in the fall of 2001, shortly after arriving at PACC, I went to a meeting of a neighborhood organization to talk to them about our antieviction work. The turnout was small, with only five or six folks sitting around a table accustomed to holding much larger groups. At the meeting I was introduced to a woman named Enida, who was somehow able to keep her newborn son DaMel quiet throughout the duration of the event.

I immediately sensed, walking home from the meeting, that Enida might be a key neighborhood leader. She was obviously intelligent, genuinely angry, and eager to do something about the problems she saw in the neighborhood. Yet it was equally clear that she had never been an engaged member of the community before and had little idea of how to achieve the goals she had set for herself.

I arranged a one-on-one meeting with Enida, where I found out more about her background. She had lived for most of her life in the Walt Whitman Public Housing complex in Fort Greene, Brooklyn, and her biggest concern was that this housing would eventually become privatized. This was the catalyst for her initial interest, and she told me that she had spent the last two months dashing off letter after letter to political representatives and public housing administrators, without receiving any responses that clarified what was going on. I invited her to an upcoming workshop focusing on public housing issues and a few weeks later asked her to chair our first monthly community meeting.

In preparation for the community meeting, Enida and I developed an agenda and role-played how she would open the meeting. She became a bit nervous (as did I) when we learned that a television channel was going to film the event for a news story on our organization's antieviction activities. But after a few meetings to make sure we were completely prepared for the evening, Enida's (and my) excitement outweighed any feelings of nervousness.

The meeting went as planned, with Enida doing a fine job of both welcoming the group and pitching membership at the end to the thirty people gathered. We were both excited to watch the television coverage, and in the weeks that followed Enida became increasingly active—helping publicize PACC's work in her public housing development and at the community board. A few months later we held a direct action targeting the predatory lending practices of New York City banks, which landed Enida and her son on the cover of a newspaper. Neighbors were stopping Enida on the street and saying that they had seen the photo, and she began to see herself as a neighborhood leader.

As Enida became more involved with PACC, I looked for something that could deepen her understanding of organizing and asked if she'd be interested in taking a class at the (sadly now defunct) New York City Organizing Support Center on the basic principles of organizing. She said yes, and from then on she would often pop into the office to share some newly gathered information about the Black Panthers or ask questions about an organization that she had heard of for the first time in class. The class also introduced her to a method of organizing— confrontational direct action—that was more impatiently aggressive than letter writing.

After being an active leader, Enida eventually became a full-time organizer at PACC for several years, focusing on tenant rights and antidisplacement organizing. She recently switched jobs after moving out of the neighborhood and is now working for another nonprofit organization in New York City.

With Enida, a slow but steady progression ensued: one-on-one meeting; invitation to a relevant workshop; chairing of a membership meeting; engaging in direct actions. While organizing, it pays to always keep your eyes and ears open, because you never know where you'll find people who may turn into dedicated leaders. I met Enida at a poorly attended night meeting, after all—a meeting that I barely to managed to attend.

Enrique: Waiting to Be Discovered

Enrique was a Mexican immigrant who, by the time we met, had already dealt with the severe lead poisoning of his daughter due to poor housing conditions.*

Any organizer with half a brain would have realized immediately upon meeting Enrique that he could become a fabulous leader. He was brash and outspoken, but within just a few minutes of conversation he also revealed a sophisticated political consciousness (like many taxi drivers, Enrique was a newshound who seemed to know about every major political development before anyone else). He lived in a building with hundreds of violations and was in the midst of suing his landlord in housing court— which had not yielded any results so far.

I invited Enrique to a legal clinic, which was of little use to him. The lawyer didn't have any new information to share that Enrique didn't already know. Despite the lack of help, Enrique

---

* I wrote about Enrique's life in detail in my first book, *There's No José Here: Following the Hidden Lives of Mexican Immigrants* (Nation Books, 2007).

still began attending our membership meetings and over the next four years—despite dealing with numerous family and housing emergencies—remained an active leader. As a Mexican immigrant, he was able to rally the immigrant community, recruit Mexicans to PACC while driving them around in his cab, and counsel them one-on-one when their landlords threatened to call immigration and have them deported.

When things got serious—for example, when we met with commissioners at the departments of Health or Housing—Enrique was always present and confident. He was a gifted public speaker, didn't become nervous in front of the television cameras, and was forever cajoling others into making sacrifices for the benefit of the neighborhood.

The reader may wonder: Where is the leadership development in Enrique's story? In truth, there wasn't much. At times I helped Enrique prepare public testimony or chair a meeting and sometimes I disagreed with him about the most effective tactics to use on specific campaigns. But he taught me at least as much about politics and leadership as I taught him. I've included Enrique's story here to remind future organizers of two things. First, in every organization one will find leaders like Enrique, who join not primarily because they want individual help but because they want to fight. Second, for these kinds of people, the main task for an organizer is to discover them. Before I ran into Enrique over a burrito in a Mexican restaurant, he was the same person: opinionated, political, of an activist mind-set. But he hadn't been asked to join an organization where he could use those skills. For folks like Enrique, all one has to do is ask.

Jedidah and the New York City Council

Jedidah was in her junior year of high school when we first met. She was one of a dozen or so high school students we worked with to test homes for lead in an environmental-justice campaign (covered in detail in the following chapter), and I was first struck by her because she was, well, quiet. She was the first to arrive at the two meetings that we held, and while many of the high school students were prone to joking around and offering their opinions without hesitation, Jedidah mostly remained silent and listened to others.

Many people's natural reaction to others who are quiet is to assume that they lack the confidence needed to lead. Being instinctively shy myself, I have always been intrigued by people who are quiet. I tried to strike up a conversation with Jedidah whenever I could, though she often answered my questions in short sentences that didn't reveal too much about what she was thinking or feeling.

On one of the last days when we went out to test homes, I purposely arranged to be in a small group with Jedidah so that I would have a chance to talk to her and see if she might be interested in continuing to be involved with PACC beyond our initial project. In the homes, while talking to parents about the problem of lead poisoning, I saw a new side of Jedidah emerge. She was very engaging and took the time to really listen to the concerns of the families whose homes we were in. At the end of the day I asked her if she enjoyed the work and might want to continue. Her eyes lit up, and she immediately said yes.

Over the summer, Jedidah interned at PACC and accomplished a great deal. As well as being a good listener, she was also a great writer and wrote a piece about her experiences working with families affected by lead poisoning that was published as an op-ed in the *New York Daily News*. After being published in a major daily newspaper (at the age of sixteen!), her confidence level rose, and she helped us plan direct actions, conduct outreach in the neighborhood, and contact other high schools to recruit students for future projects. Toward the end of the summer, the City Council was holding a second hearing on stronger lead legislation, and Jedidah decided to testify.

While we worked on her testimony, I tried to reassure her that she was going to do a great job and that it was quite all right to be nervous. I told her, in all honesty, that I would have been scared to death to be testifying in front of politicians at City Hall and that I admired her for her courage. Not surprisingly, she did a wonderful job, and her testimony was widely praised—even by the chair of the committee, who was steadfastly against the bill. In her testimony she recounted her experiences in Bedford-Stuyvesant:

> The lead project not only enabled me to learn about the problem at hand, but to aid in addressing it. Going into the homes of potentially lead-poisoned children was a difficult but necessary task. We found that at least one-third of the homes were neglected. There was chipped and deteriorated paint, water damage, and lead levels that were beyond dangerous. I was appalled that such homes had toddlers and preschoolers in them. I was shocked that many of the children had not been tested for lead and that before we came the parents had not even known that their child was at risk. . . . Going out into the community to apply the skills that I learned has been very meaningful. I am inspired to continue fighting to heal the wounds caused by the many problems in society. This experience has convinced me that if the great minds—young and old—come together within our community we can bring about change.

After the hearing Jedidah continued to work at PACC, eventually as a part-time paid youth organizer. Again, Jedidah reminded me—as did Enida and Enrique—that leadership development must begin with a belief that "ordinary" people, people who may be regularly passed over because they are immigrants, or poor, or shy, or young, have hidden abilities. It is the organizer's job to encourage such people and to remain steadfastly skeptical of the claim that only a few can lead. In doing so, we'll also gain confidence from the leaders we identify—I certainly did from Enida, Enrique, and Jedidah—and in this way we also develop new skills and emerge into leaders as well—though leaders who are committed to developing leadership in others. It is a wonderful job.

THE ESSENTIAL FINDING

The author Carol Bly, in her thought-provoking and inspiring book on ethical behavior and human development, *Changing the Bully Who Rules the World*, writes that:

> *The recent good news . . . is inestimably beautiful: it is that there are no prototypes such as "natural leaders" and "natural followers." There are people in whom psychological and cognitive growth have received this much encouragement and people whose psychological and cognitive growth have only received that much encouragement, but the essential and democratic finding is that what were once loosely called "leadership qualities" are part of the formula for every member of the species.*[20]

This "essential and democratic finding"—that leadership qualities in fact exist in all of us—is a rewording of sorts of the Industrial Workers of the World slogan "We Are All Leaders!" It has also become shorthand for my philosophy on leadership development. By keeping this essential finding in mind, we recognize the untapped potential and unrealized talent that may exist just below the surface—both in ourselves as organizers and in the community residents with whom we work. It is a generous, hopeful, and optimistic way of looking at the world and yet it is also practical and realistic. I have seen people like Enida, Enrique, Jedidah, and many others emerge into people who take on new leadership roles and create new images of themselves when given the support and encouragement needed. The essential finding, I have decided, is not only pleasant and inspiring but accurate as well.

Chapter 5

GOT A PROBLEM? PROVE IT!

Using Research to Support Your Organizing

You are morally entitled to 100 percent and legally entitled to 95 percent of the information you are seeking. People who refuse to give it to you can be legitimately and publicly asked, "What are you trying to hide?"
—Kim Bobo, Jackie Kendall, and Steve Max[1]

In high school I had a certain teacher who loved to hand out worksheets. We'd do three or four sheets of fill-in-the-blank material in every class, and the teacher's faith in the format was so rock solid that it didn't even matter whether or not the topics on the worksheet actually corresponded to the class lesson. These were worksheets, so we did them—in no particular order, with no particular rationale.

I would usually breeze through the problems at about a 50 percent accuracy clip and during the remaining time write sarcastic little thoughts to myself about the inanity of worksheets in general. I would, of course, always erase my own contribution before handing in the papers, but one day this step eluded me. So after turning in a sheet that had my own commentary intact, I was called in the next day to have a discussion with the teacher. She was eager to help me alleviate my distaste for worksheets. Instead, I was told, I would from that day on turn in a three-page report for each worksheet that was assigned. The teacher gave me the "privilege" of doing research on specific topics (and no, she explained, I could not come up with my own topics). Though I don't remember turning in very many subsequent reports for her, I still developed a strong predilection against doing research of any kind.

Ironically, as an organizer I found myself doing research of some sort almost every day. Of course, this research is of a different nature and done for a different purpose. Research by organizers is conducted for many reasons: to discover problems that are affecting communities where one is organizing and give voice to previously ignored members; to understand our targets' vulnerabilities; to achieve media coverage; to legitimize campaigns; and to push through policy solutions. Such research can be used to orient and propel organizing campaigns and should be thought of as a weapon in the arsenal of the community organizer.

It bears mention, however, that research is only as useful as an organization makes it; frequently, after hours of painstaking research, reports and other documents end up doing nothing more than collecting dust. Research, then, must be connected to campaigns of action to be useful. It is a critical piece of the puzzle but not the answer to the puzzle itself. Conducting research without grassroots action is for think tanks and academic institutions. Holding actions and campaigns without research, on the other hand, will always fail to gain the results we could have achieved had we done our homework.

THE MISCONCEPTIONS OF RESEARCH

For readers who are in high school or college or have recently graduated and have fresh memories of struggling through mind-draining research to crank out a last-minute fifteen-page paper on a topic that held no interest: I understand the instinctive lack of enthusiasm you may have about talking about research. But that type of dry and disconnected research is not at all what we are talking about.

First of all, research for organizing purposes is not conducted objectively. As Kim Bobo, Jackie Kendall, and Steve Max write in their book *Organize!* "the word 'research' often implies knowledge divorced from action. In the academic world, one is expected to approach a research project with an open mind, free of preconceived ideas or values."[2] But as organizers, though we should, of course, have open minds, we approach the topic of research with a very biased agenda formed by a simple preconception: there are a lot of terrible things going on out there due to a lot of terrible policies. Research can help organizers understand exactly what is going on, what is wrong with what is going on, what would be a better alternative, and how best to get to that alternative.

Second, organizing research frequently has enjoyable results. For example, much time is spent trying to figure out imaginative ways to expose established targets. I attended one protest held in front of a landlord's house that was organized by a community organization called the Fifth Avenue Committee (FAC). Organizers at FAC had dreamed up a plan to hold a fund-raising dinner on the lawn in front of the house of a landlord who was evicting a senior citizen, complete with dozens of chairs, numerous folding tables, tablecloths, and enough silverware and food to serve fifty people. We parked in front of the house in two yellow school buses, rapidly pulled out and arranged the equipment, and sat down at the makeshift dinner table for a feast of rice and beans. While we ate, people went door-to-door, soliciting donations from neighbors while explaining that the funds raised would help keep a vulnerable tenant in her home.

The point is that organizers can get creative with their research. The organizers at FAC had researched where the landlord lived, brainstormed the idea of a fund-raiser, gotten together all of the necessary supplies, looked at what fund-raising dinners usually entailed, and scoped out the actual location to make sure they could pull it off. A far cry from the boring research my high school teacher had demanded of me—and it proved to be a good time for both the organizers and the members who participated.

Third, organizing research is usually based upon actually talking with others and, as Rinku Sen writes, using "people as primary sources."[3] Researchers are generally thought of as people with PhDs who pore over arcane documents and read through all types of dense publications, hardly ever speaking to another soul about their project. But in organizing, research involves working extensively with the affected community to discover what problems people are experiencing and relying upon this information as the primary source for all research endeavors. When we are organizing in specific neighborhoods or around specific issues, the people in question—whether restaurant workers, families on public assistance, or people living with disabilities—have a valuable contribution to make to the debate, and we can use research to place their experiences front and center.

This chapter looks at the general types of research that organizers regularly use, from tactical research and power analysis to community-based or, as it is sometimes called, participatory action research. With each type of research I give examples from my time in Brooklyn—and with participatory research I include a detailed case study of an environmental-justice campaign we conducted that focused on lead poisoning. This project used high school students trained in an

Environmental Protection Agency (EPA)–certified workshop as researchers who tested homes for lead dust; the project is examined closely to show the different types of research that were critical to our work and helped inform our campaign direction and the demands we made to New York City officials and politicians.

TACTICAL RESEARCH: KNOW THINE ENEMY

Tactical research, whether about targets or policies, is critical to organizing. One of the first things we would do in Brooklyn, when confronted with a new eviction that we were thinking of organizing against, was to discover as much information as possible about the landlord. Did he own other properties? If so, how many and where? Did these properties have many building violations? Did he own other businesses? Was the landlord rich? What were the mortgage payments on the building where the eviction was taking place? Such questions helped us understand whether the landlord was a small homeowner just trying to get enough money to make his or her mortgage payments or a large-scale speculator unconcerned with anything but maximizing profit.

If we were going to go after the landlord and escalate the conflict, we needed to know more. Where did the landlord live? Work? Worship? Relax? Such information helped lay the framework for the campaign and enabled us to know which buttons to push to get what we wanted.★

Tactical research about policies is equally important: Since we are trying to change current policies, we'd better know what's wrong with them and be able to posit something better. Screaming about a disastrous policy or law is only half the struggle; we've got to be able to develop thoughtful solutions so that we have an

---

★ At times all we would need to do to find out most of these questions was to Google the target on the Internet.

answer to the inevitable question: "Well, do you have a better idea?" If we're not prepared to answer with a resounding "Yes!" and follow it up with a proposal, then we've failed, giving our opponents the opportunity to write us off as crazy citizens who just like to complain about everything under the sun.

When doing tactical research on targets and policies, grassroots groups may at times choose to partner with another organization that specializes in research to obtain hard-to-find information. In Brooklyn I was fortunate in that I had a number of friends working as researchers for labor unions and could always count on them to pull up information on targets when I'd hit a dead end on my own. Unions, with their relatively large budgets, generally have research staff to complement their organizing efforts. But most grassroots organizations do not have the funding capacity to hire individuals whose sole job is to conduct research. Therefore they have to decide when it is appropriate to partner with a research organization to accomplish their goals. This is something that has to be decided more or less on a case-by-case basis.

Every now and then, when digging around for information on targets, an organizer hits pay dirt. While we were working with a coalition to push through a stronger lead-poisoning prevention bill, a city councilmember from Brooklyn who sat on the Housing and Buildings Committee, Kendell Stewart, was proving to be a major adversary. He regularly made comments about how the biggest problem was that immigrants were coming to New York City already poisoned (an awkward position to take, since Stewart was an immigrant himself) and that landlords already carried too heavy a burden.

Acting on a tip from an ally, I spent one late afternoon at Brooklyn's housing court searching through case records until I found the index number that I was looking for, a case where Stewart himself had been taken to court by a tenant of a building he owned. Pulling the file, I discovered that Stewart had been fined $27,000 for not providing heat and hot water, along with numerous citations of lead-paint violations. But when Stewart, after being slapped with the fine, came to court to speak to the judge, the court papers showed that his penalty was reduced by $26,700 to a single fee of $300—with no explanation.

I found out this information on a Friday afternoon, with the first City Council hearing on the lead-paint bill scheduled for Monday morning. I brought the file to the third floor, where a few copy machines were located, but digging through my pockets, I realized that I had no money—not even a dime—on me. For a moment I panicked; I needed to make copies of the documents to have a story. By scavenging around in the halls of housing court, I managed to pull together seventy-five cents from security guards. Fifteen minutes before closing time, I walked out with five sheets of paper that, if used correctly, could be explosive.

When I got back to the office, I called our communications firm, which suggested I pitch the story to a friendly reporter who covered the City Hall beat for the *New York Daily News*. Within minutes I was speaking to the reporter, who—after having the court papers faxed over to her—demanded that I not tell a soul. I didn't.

On Monday morning a story broke—anonymously (though PACC did get a quote in)—about a City councilmember who was opposing stronger lead-paint legislation and who owned a building with numerous violations, including peeling lead paint. Digging himself into a deeper hole, Stewart had argued to the reporter that the poor building conditions were due to Haitian tenants, whose "cultural differences" were to blame. This interesting explanation—that people from a tropical climate would choose to spend New York City winters bathing their children in frigid water—was a difficult one to defend. But defend it he did, arriving late to the hearing because he was fielding questions from reporters for over an hour about the possibility that he was a Haitian-bashing slumlord.

During the remainder of the hearing he stayed quiet, though when he did attempt to make an incoherent comment, he was roundly booed by the audience. Through a little bit of lucky research, the opposition had been neutralized.

At times, then, tactical research can end up being pretty interesting, and organizers may feel like private eyes when they are scouting out a proposed location for a demonstration or searching through public records in hopes of finding something damaging. My most memorable experiences conducting tactical research—though I never engaged in this while in Brooklyn—was "dumpster diving" (or OB, as it was called in Spanish, meaning *operación basura*—operation garbage), where we would clandestinely go through a corporation's trash to discover potentially important information. Though the legality of this move is suspect, it has often yielded valuable information—and it always got my blood pumping when I was scaling barbed wire fences at four in the morning.★

Suffice it to say, when organizers engage in tactical research, they are bound to get themselves into interesting and unfamiliar situations—which should be enjoyed whenever they present themselves.

Power Analysis:
Who Can Give You What You Want?

Imagine that you're trying to improve the long waits in welfare offices, and you want to pass a law mandating more funds for hiring caseworkers. Your city councilmember is on record as stating that welfare recipients are "lazy drug addicts" and that he doesn't believe funds should be made available to hire more workers. You plan a direct action in front of the councilmember's office, attracting plenty of media. After an hour of your chanting, he finally emerges, and your group confronts him, demanding that he vote in support of the proposed legislation.

"I'd love to," he says, a disingenuous look of contrition on his face. "But unfortunately, you're talking to the wrong guy. That's a federal issue—I can't do anything about it."

★ I'm not advocating engaging in illegal maneuvers, just reporting the honest facts. Organizers have to define their own ethical code. For me, to break the law a bit in the fight to challenge employers that routinely break the law to exploit their workers—well, let's just say I've never lost a moment of sleep over it.

Of course, the councilmember may be lying; the first defense targets usually come up with is to shift responsibility to someone else. But we should always know that the person who we're targeting actually has the means to pull off what we're demanding, were they to make our demand a priority. There's no sense in beating up on the wrong person. If you're organizing around a federal issue, city and state politicians may be able to offer their support but they're not the ultimate deciders. Know who can give you what you want.

Unions have become especially adept at conducting sophisticated power analyses in their campaigns, prodding around with a spear before finding the dragon's soft spot. When I was organizing on the Justice for Janitors campaign in Denver as a participant in the Union Summer program (for more information about Union Summer, see the Resources and Opportunities section), we were seeking to force a cleaning contractor to allow its workers to unionize. The primary target was, then, the contractor. But, as unions across the country have found out, contractors can be very difficult targets. Their workforce is often transient and undocumented, which makes them harder to organize. So strategists decided to shift the focus to include the property managers that were hiring the contractors. If property managers were pressured to hire unionized janitors, then the contractor would either have to allow their workers to unionize or lose valuable contracts.

But how to pressure property managers? They're usually large owners of corporate complexes and upscale malls, whose tenants include law firms, trendy microbreweries, and other white-collar offices. They contract with nonunionized firms to clean their buildings because it saves them money. But they also depend upon tenants that are satisfied with their management. A rowdy group of protesters could scare away customers seeking to drink a $3 latte or choice microbrew. See where I'm heading?

Based upon this power analysis, Justice for Janitors found an opening. By asking commercial tenants to sign petitions demanding their property manager hire a unionized cleaning company, the campaign worked to pressure the manager into switching contractors. To escalate the conflict, we held direct actions in front of the buildings to disrupt the local businesses and publicize the issue. We also went office to office, explaining the situation to the tenants and asking them to sign a petition; the most sympathetic tenants would take the petition directly to the property management's office—usually in the same building—and ask for a personal response. This combination of holding disruptive actions at restaurants and bars along with steady organizing among the building's other tenants proved effective. In Denver, by the end of the summer our target had agreed to abide by a "card check" and recognize the formation of a union if a majority of employees signed a card in support (and which circumvents the frequent harassment and coercion that companies engage in during a traditional union drive that concludes with a vote). A year later, one thousand new Denver janitors became unionized.

COMMUNITY-BASED OR PARTICIPATORY ACTION RESEARCH:
Enlisting Members as Researchers

When organizers are engaged in tactical research, they are frequently working alone or with a few others in the quest to find information on targets or to study policies. But community-based research is entirely different; we are giving community members the tools needed to be researchers themselves and we go about collecting information by speaking with others and recording the results.

In addition, community-based research does more than simply collect information. The participatory-research project documented in the case study below highlights the multifaceted purposes for which research can be used: not only to discover facts but to use the process of discovering facts to develop and push an issue and identify potential leaders. For example, Rinku Sen writes that when an organization engages in community-based research, it does so for many reasons:

When we go out to survey teenagers about their recreation and job needs, or welfare applicants about their experiences, we can get names and phone numbers and go back to those people to recruit them for our campaign. They, in turn, can conduct surveys with other people. When we combine research and outreach, the conversation has to further each.[4]

Thus, though community-based research is used to discover information and eventually be able to paint an accurate picture of what is happening, for organizing it can play many additional roles, such as providing a means of conducting outreach in the community and identifying and developing leaders.

This type of research validates ordinary people's own experiences and can give them a renewed sense of their importance. For example, instead of listening to pundits talk abstractly about poverty, members can reclaim their experiences for themselves and ask others to contribute as well. Who better to engage in this research than the people directly affected by the issue? And what more accurate way to understand problems than by documenting people's actual experiences? Community-based research allows us, in Sen's words, to take back the facts and affirms that the people we are working with are also "experts" who have the special insight that can only come from individuals who have intimate knowledge about how the system works—or doesn't.

CASE STUDY IN BROOKLYN:
Using Research to Move an Environmental Justice Campaign

The following case study, which examines a real campaign that we organized in Brooklyn, is broken down into five aspects: Background

Planning, Implementation of the Project, Formulation of Demands, Releasing Information, and Aftermath. It is hoped that if we look in depth at the various aspects of the project, different research techniques and their effective use in the organizing campaign will come to life.

Background Planning

When we first began doing environmental-justice organizing around the issue of lead-paint poisoning, we had a lot of catching up to do. Many organizations in New York City had been working on childhood lead poisoning for decades, and we were the new kids on the block who were getting our hands dirty for the first time.

We needed to decide upon our campaign strategy. We knew that we were located in one of the neighborhoods that experienced the highest rate of lead poisoning, Bedford-Stuyvesant, and that the majority of the homes suffered from code violations that increased the likelihood of there being lead hazards.

Many other groups doing lead-poisoning work focused exclusively on education projects, such as holding workshops for parents on ways to minimize dangers and handing out flyers on what types of diets could protect children from lead. With all their good intentions, these activities struck us as somewhat ridiculous. Lead was in homes, the old paint was deteriorating and poisoning children, and it needed to either be removed or covered up. Education without corrective action to remove the lead hazards wasn't totally pointless, but it did seem to be the wrong path in preventing childhood lead poisoning.

With some research and assistance from Alfredo deAvila of the Center for Third World Organizing (CTWO), we discovered that it was relatively simple to become certified to test homes for lead dust, which is the primary pathway by which children are poisoned. All a person had to do was take a one-day EPA-certified course to become a "lead-sampling technician." Then, with this training and the proper supplies (which basically consisted of a glo-rified napkin used to collect the dust), we could go out and see how widespread the lead dangers really were.

After we found a trainer and supplier of the materials needed to do the tests and laboratory analysis, we met with a friendly teacher at a local high school, the Benjamin Banneker Academy, and presented our project idea. We wanted to take ten high school students from Bedford-Stuyvesant and ten PACC members through the course, and then test dozens of neighborhood homes to discover the extent of lead dangers. We explained to the teacher, Valentino Ellis, that we wanted to turn our findings into a report that could provide a snap-shot of the environmental dangers faced by the children of central Brooklyn and also profile high school student participants and parents whose children were in danger of being poisoned. Our meeting was successful. Valentino was very excited about the idea and promised that he could get a group of students who would want to take part. Our project was officially off the ground.

Implementation of the Project

To conduct the project, we had to speak to families and sign them up to have their apartments tested for lead. PACC organizers spent two months door knocking in a twelve-square-block area of Bed-ford-Stuyvesant and leafleted at neighborhood churches and schools—eventually signing up sixty families for lead tests.

After the two-month period, we held our first meeting with the high school students to discuss the project and organized an EPA-certified training so that the participants would be licensed to test homes for lead dust. Though the EPA training was tremendously boring and not all that helpful (though we did all receive our cer-tificates), we also spent a day in the field with an environmental-justice advocate, Dennis Livingston, who traveled up to Brooklyn from Baltimore for the weekend. Dennis had trained students in his hometown to test apartments, and he took our group in Brooklyn through a similar hands-on session. After visiting actual homes with Dennis and taking practice samples, our group was ready to venture out into the neighborhood and start doing some serious testing.

PACC organizers and high school students spent the next five Saturdays testing homes, and we soon had back from the lab the results for fifty-nine apartment units in thirty-five different buildings. Our findings were frightening:

- More than one third—thirteen out of thirty-five—of the buildings tested were found to have one or more apartments with hazardous amounts of lead;
- Some 32 percent—nineteen out of fifty-nine—of the individual apartments tested had dangerous amounts of lead, many with levels well in excess of EPA safety thresholds. We found apartments with lead levels anywhere from five to one hundred times the EPA threshold;
- And 89 percent of these hazardous apartments housed children under six, an age when their rapid development makes them most susceptible to permanent brain damage and their frequent hand-to-mouth activity means they are likely to ingest flaking paint fragments and dust.

We held a community meeting with the families to hand out the individual results and summarize our findings, which demonstrated that many of the neighborhood children were threatened. Before the meeting, we sat down with a few parent leaders who were discovered to have lead hazards to discuss the results and ask if they would share their feelings with the group and lead a discussion about what type of collective action we could take to fix the crisis. The meeting went well, and many parents—though anxious about their individual situations—were angry and ready to speak out about the issue to bring change. They felt that our approach—creating a report to publicize our findings and make policy recommendations—was a good one. Many agreed to attend a future press conference to release the report.

Our findings on lead meant that we had a story, but we still needed to do the research to formulate our demands. The campaign would be strengthened by our discovery of widespread lead dangers, and we had parents who were motivated to push for change, but the question we needed to answer was: what policy changes needed to occur?

Formulation of Demands

The intensive door knocking and outreach we had conducted helped us develop relationships with scores of new families, many of whom discovered that they lived in dangerous housing and sub-sequently became that much more involved and outraged. PACC organizer Hector Rivera and I conducted numerous follow-up visits to hear the experiences and concerns of the families and explain to them some of the goals we hoped to achieve. Based on the information discovered by PACC's campaign researcher, Amy Laura Cahn, and meetings with residents, we formulated three policy changes as the demands of the report.

Demand Number 1: *The Department of Health must drop its definition of lead poisoning, in accordance with medical research, from 20 micrograms per deciliter to 5 micrograms*

A mother named Abby invited us in immediately when we were door knocking; she had spent the previous year worried about her son's blood lead level but couldn't get the Department of Health (DOH) to do anything to assist her. Her son's level was 18 micrograms per deciliter, then 14, and had finally dropped down to 9 (research has shown that dramatic drops in IQ occur at levels between 5 and 10). He had been poisoned for over a year.

"I called the Department of Health," she told us. "But they

told me that they couldn't help yet, that his numbers weren't high enough. They said, 'wait a little while, and maybe they'll go up.' But I didn't want them to go up!"

Abby's frustration pointed to a policy failure of the DOH: the department considered a child "poisoned" when she tested at a level of 20 or above on the first test or 15 to 19 for two consecutive tests with at least ninety days apart. Even though medical research has shown that levels below 10 can cause negative impacts on the development of children, the DOH's regulations meant that the agency wouldn't take immediate corrective action, for example, in the case of a child with a level of 19. Instead, the parent would have to wait three months before receiving another test, which would mean that the child remained in the hazardous apartment during the ninety-day period, risking further exposure to lead.

Strengthening our case, a groundbreaking report was published in the *New England Journal of Medicine* while we were finishing up our lead tests, linking even extremely low levels of exposure to dramatic drops in IQ.

Demand Number 2: *The Department of Health must undertake a massive effort to screen children*

While door knocking and testing apartments for lead, we surveyed families on some basic background information, including whether or not their children had been tested for lead. We discovered that many families had children who had never been screened and that virtually no parents whose kids *had* been screened actually knew the results.

In addition to this personal information given by neighborhood residents, Amy Laura also looked at the DOH's own statistics on childhood lead screening. Its numbers further corroborated our own door-to-door survey results. According to the DOH, only 27 percent of New York City children were being tested, as required by law, at both ages one and two. With our own neighborhood results and official agency admission of failure, our second demand was that the DOH undergo a massive effort to screen children by sending out educational information to all medical providers, requiring that regulations be posted in waiting rooms, and reinstating mobile screening units throughout high-risk communities.

Demand Number 3: *Both the Department of Housing Preservation and Development and the Department of Health must begin targeting high-risk neighborhoods with regular inspections*

The third demand focused on the need for the City to inspect buildings aggressively in neighborhoods where children were at a high risk for lead poisoning. On their own, the agencies weren't going to initiate such a task, but a piece of pending citywide legislation, Intro 101a, stated specifically that the agencies needed to create a proposal for proactively inspecting apartments in high-risk neighborhoods and use certified workers to remove lead hazards (the current bill allowed untrained workers to do the abatement, which often only made the situation worse by stirring up lead dust.) So this demand folded itself neatly into the ongoing movement for stronger legislation and enforcement.

Releasing Information

For three weeks we worked on putting together the report, entitled "The Politics of Poison: Why One Out of Three Bedford-Stuyvesant Children Are Growing Up in Housing That Impairs Their Cognitive Development." The report had an executive summary outlining our findings and recommendations as well as personal testimonies from parents and students involved in the project.★

★ A useful book on writing effective reports is *Spinworks: A Media Guidebook for Communicating Values and Shaping Opinions* by Robert Bray.

The first thing I did was to pitch the study to a friendly reporter at the *New York Times,* who agreed to run the story in exchange for an exclusive.* We sent her an early copy of the report and connected her with the families that were profiled.

We decided to release the report on the steps of Brooklyn's Borough Hall (sort of an equivalent of Manhattan's City Hall for Brooklyn), and hold the press conference at midmorning on a Monday. Monday is generally a slow news day, and a midmorning press conference would allow reporters ample time to interview affected parents in their homes and follow up with City officials for the evening news broadcasts.

Hector and I prepped four parents for the press conference, helping them develop their public testimony. On the Monday morning of our press conference, as scheduled, the *Times* ran a story on our project, entitled "One in Three Children in Part of Brooklyn Exposed to Lead Dangers, Study Finds." The article outlined our findings, listed the three policy recommendations of our report, and quoted parents who were found to be living in dangerous housing. It struck exactly the tone we were hoping for.

Our press conference that day was a success. Every major English and Spanish television network in New York City showed up and covered the event, and three other newspapers ran stories the following day. PACC members were interviewed on four different radio stations as well, and within the next month, two more articles were written on the study in community papers. Jedidah, as mentioned in the previous chapter, even had an op-ed published in the *Daily News.*

---

* An exclusive is granted to a reporter—giving them sole access to a story—to allow them to "break" the story. Especially for stories that involve a lot of background information and/or substantial reports to be digested, it is generally wise for the organizer to grant an exclusive.

Aftermath

On the Friday before our Monday press conference, PACC had called the Department of Housing Preservation and Development (HPD) to give them fair warning about our study. PACC had a contract with HPD for various housing activities (though of course not our lead work), and it seemed only decent to allow them a bit of time to prepare for the release of our report.

HPD's response, predictably, was one of outrage—though not about the state of lead hazards in Brooklyn but about the fact that we conducted the project without the department's prior approval. I received an e-mail from one of the PR people that I saved just for fun:

> *What concerns us is those 20 apartments with children under six found to contain dangerous levels of lead. If you were a doctor or a building owner, you would be required by law to report those apartments; as an advocacy group, we believe you are morally obligated to report them so we can inspect and initiate the corrective process. According to your study results, there are children at risk. Please call 311 immediately (the City's information number) and register a complaint for those apartments.*

Despite such strong words and moral suasion, PACC refused to release the information to HPD because we had an agreement with the parents to hand over the results collectively in a face-to-face meeting with HPD officials.★ HPD arranged for us to meet with their head of code enforcement a few days after our press

---

★ It should be noted that HPD's concern about the well-being of the families and desire to act immediately to protect them diminished over time. Though they were outraged that we were going to wait three days to give them the addresses—apparently uneasy about the idea that the families would have to spend the weekend living in danger—six months later we were still waiting for them to finish abating the lead from one of the apartments, where a two-year old girl had been poisoned.

conference. At the meeting we handed over the addresses of the apartments with lead, and parents told them directly that their policies were failing to protect children. When Enrique, a father of a lead-poisoned child, demanded that HPD inspect every building in the neighborhood, he was told that this would be "impossible." From that day on, whenever referring to a problem with HPD, Enrique would break into a grin and mutter *impossible* over and over again, appreciating the incompetence of the agency.

Just days later, we heard from our members that numerous inspectors had visited their apartments and had written up citations for dozens of lead-paint violations. As we continued to monitor the individual cases, some landlords came forward to do the repairs; in the cases of others who were not responsive (a large majority), HPD eventually came in and completed the work, billing the landlord.

Two weeks after our report was released, City Council held a hearing on new lead legislation, Intro 101a. The hearing had been scheduled months earlier, and while planning the production and release of our report, we were careful to make sure we would have it ready well before the hearing date. At the hearing, City Council representatives and City Comptroller William Thompson cited our report as evidence that the current law was not adequate. Other City councilmembers were carrying our report (we had sent it out to all of them a week earlier) as they demanded answers from representatives of the housing and health agencies. The report offered irrefutable proof that the current legislation was not doing enough to protect New York City children.

In the end, our participatory-research project accomplished some immediate and predictable goals, and there were some positive developments that we hadn't anticipated. Suddenly many residents of Bedford-Stuyvesant were talking about the danger of lead poisoning and were taking their children in to get tested. The families that were found to have dangerous lead levels in their homes were able to get needed repairs, preventing their children from further exposure. Some of these parents became leaders on the issue, speaking to the press, testifying before City Council, and demanding action from officials. Students learned that they could play a critical role in protecting the health of neighborhood children and many became politicized through their work, wanting to continue to work for social justice in one capacity or another in the future. Our project also added momentum to the push for stronger City legislation: in the winter of 2004, the City Council voted to pass Intro 101a, creating the most protective lead bill in the nation.

There were also some unexpected developments. As a result of the press coverage, a nurse contacted us about holding community screening days in local churches, and we were able to test at-risk children, many of whom had no health insurance and had gone untested. We met with several local groups looking to set up similar programs to test homes in their neighborhood, and we fielded calls from places as far away as North Carolina and Georgia.

Also, by doing research and releasing the report, our organization became known as an expert of sorts in the field of lead. Reporters would regularly call us when anything dealing with lead entered the news, and with this development we found ourselves in the press more and more. We also received many calls from community residents looking to get involved with our organization and were able to recruit new leaders to help build our organization.

Lastly, our pilot project laid the groundwork for a youth organizing project that continues today and includes a curriculum on environmental justice and training in organizing techniques for high school students. Through the publicity of the original project we were able to raise enough funds to run youth organizing training sessions twice a year and continue to test more than a hundred apartment units for lead annually. Slowly we are making the neighborhood of Bedford-Stuyvesant free from lead hazards block by block and training parents and high school students to become neighborhood leaders active in the struggle to protect the right of children to grow up in conditions free from the damaging effects of lead.

FINAL THOUGHT:
The Limits of Research

Learning how to conduct research is a critical skill for community organizers, but it must always be remembered that research by itself can only accomplish so much. Never in the history of the world has it been easier to access such a wide range of information on an infinite number of topics. But facts alone do not change the world. Having decided what type of data is needed, organizers engage in research to find and use such information in campaigns of *action*. Without such an emphasis on action, research will be conducted within a vacuum and will only lead to yet more "perfect" reports that move quickly onto bookshelves and are forgotten, having little to no impact on attempts to eliminate the documented injustices.

That being said, without doing research, organizers face serious limitations in their work, forced simply to react to immediate problems without seeking long-term solutions. We need to know about our targets and their points of vulnerability, about policies that fail and how they can be fixed, about what types of problems are affecting the members of the communities in which we are organizing. By dedicating substantial time to conducting research, we acknowledge that our work is part of a larger picture and we become better able to run informed campaigns that take this larger picture into account.

Chapter 6

DEMYSTIFYING THE MEDIA:

Getting the Coverage Your Issue Deserves

When I first began organizing in Brooklyn, I was quite intimidated by the prospect of interacting with the media. I had no idea what a press release was, and whenever a reporter called fishing for a story, my stomach would tighten and I'd stammer while trying to think up something intelligent to say.

This early intimidation now seems ironic, because while there are many thorny and complicated aspects of organizing—which remain challenging regardless of the amount of experience one has—working with the media seems by far the easiest to understand. What fueled my anxiety was simply that I didn't know *anything* about how the media functioned, or what reporters looked for, or how to write a press release. It all seemed so mysterious; now it seems almost mundane. In this chapter, I hope to take some of the mystery out of working with the media, so that organizers can better understand how to achieve coverage as they move campaigns forward.

Achieving media coverage is important for a number of reasons. It can expose and embarrass targets and highlight problems that push policy makers into a corner, forcing them to act upon something they previously ignored. It allows members the chance to develop new leadership skills as they become public actors and injects a deeper sense of importance into the organization's work. Finally, it allows foundations and other potential supporters a chance to see that your organization is having an impact. Though media coverage should not be viewed as something that "legitimizes" a group, in the eyes of funders (and politicians) this is unfortunately too often the case. The good news is that once one learns how to think like a reporter, the task of achieving coverage becomes much more manageable.

THE MOST FREQUENT MEDIA INTERACTION:
Holding an Action

Before going into detail about how to work with the media, let's first outline the most common scenario that organizers will have to deal with, which is publicizing an event—usually a protest. The mechanics are easy enough to grasp and after a few actions they will seem pretty formulaic.

Let's say that we're going to protest in front of a supermarket where workers haven't been paid by management. Our members, the workers, choose to hold a picket line in front of the store at noon on a Saturday, when many people will be shopping. We go over the talking points that we want to focus on and perhaps select a few workers to do the bulk of the speaking to the media.

Once these parameters are set, the next thing to do is to write up a media advisory that explains the event in clear terms. This goes out to media outlets usually a few days before the event, probably on a Thursday or Friday morning for an action scheduled for Saturday. The advisory states the basic facts of the event clearly, listing time, date, contact information, the basic story line of the event, and any notable items—such as visuals—that will be included.

After the advisory goes out (by fax and, increasingly, e-mail), an organizer then follows up with phone calls to make sure that the outlets received the document and to pitch the event. The pitch has to be quick and compelling. Then, on the morning of the event, one sends out the press release, which is usually written in the past tense and features a quote or two from the participants—the supermarket workers, in this case. (Some media outlets are quite small and may not be able to send a reporter to the event but can follow up via phone and insert the quotes you've included in the release for their story. I've had community papers print our press releases verbatim as stories.)

By the morning of the event, an organizer has, you hope, received a few calls from media outlets that are interested in coming. At the supermarket, the organizer brings the press releases to hand out, as well as some basic information about the organization,* and as the group chants in the picket line, the designated workers speak to the cameras and the print journalists about their experiences. That night, if all goes well, you're on the local news, and the next morning you wake to find sympathetic stories in the papers.

That, stated concisely, is the most frequent media interaction that organizers have. Yet, of course, there's a bunch of finer points to keep in mind.

---

* Some people have told me that it's important to have thorough press packets that include all kinds of information about the organization. Though this doesn't cause any harm, I've never actually had anything come of it. Reporters, especially TV reporters, move from story to story so quickly that usually they'll never even read the literature. I gave up on fancy press packets long ago, unless the event promises to truly solicit massive media coverage.

GOOD VERSUS EVIL:
The Need for a Moral Conflict

Let's say you're working on a critical issue that affects thousands of people. You've spent months planning an event to highlight the problem and are anticipating substantial media coverage. Yet on the day of the action, no one shows. What gives?

There is always the possibility that something happened that day in the world that pushed out everything else (we held a great event on the same day that the United States began its invasion of Iraq and got zero coverage). But if this isn't the case, then the likely problem is that you forgot about the most basic ingredient of a successful event: a moral conflict.

An enticing news story is one that has a fight between the forces of good (you) and the forces of evil (your target). Organizers have to be able to frame their events in these terms, promising a collision of two opposing groups. Reporters are not going to be interested in our work for its own sake—a lesson it took me some time to learn. So it is the organizer's task to demonstrate that although many different events are occurring on a given day, our event promises to be especially compelling and dramatic.

For example, let's imagine that rats are overrunning a neighborhood. Residents are upset and plan a press conference in front of one of the homes of a community leader, where families will speak about the need to work together to get rid of the rats. Is this newsworthy?

Perhaps, if it's a slow news day. But what the story lacks is a target and hence a moral angle (not to mention that it doesn't fit into any organizing campaign). For one thing, who's to blame for the rats—the community because it has been insufficiently involved? An outlet might hesitate to cover the event simply because no one wants to see a bunch of neighbors complaining to themselves about their problem. In many urban areas, rats seem to be a fact of life. Nothing interesting here.

But organizers would think about the problem in another way. Why are the rats everywhere? Usually, it's because trash isn't being picked up and rats have access to buffet-style meals at all hours of the day. It's the Sanitation Department's job to pick up the trash, and if they picked it up more regularly, the rat population would definitely decrease. In addition, if a landlord isn't storing the garbage properly, then it's the Sanitation Department's job to slap some hefty fines on the landlord. Now we've got a story.

Instead of holding a press conference to "come together," residents would be better served by staging a demonstration in front of the home of the head of the Sanitation Department, bringing dead rats to his or her doorstep and demanding immediate action. Chances are good that the target lives in a pretty decent house where rats aren't a problem. This juxtaposition will frame the issue and intrigue reporters. The story is easy to understand, it has some conflict (Jerry Springer knew what he was doing), and it has a human-interest story that people can relate to (distant bureaucrats ignoring the needs of ordinary people). In addition, the protest has the benefit of unpredictability. Will the head of the Sanitation Department be home? If so, what will his or her reaction be? Reporters know that unscripted conflicts like this can make for great television, since they'll get the chance to ring the doorbell of the commissioner's home and play the role of crusading journo.

WHO SPEAKS TO THE MEDIA?

For most organizations and corporations, the question of who speaks to the media is one of PR and hierarchy. CEOs are accustomed to weighing in on issues, and whole departments are employed in the service of manipulation—especially when reacting to events that cast a corporation in a negative light. These large corporations exist to further their own specific agenda and so they put much effort into developing a strict hierarchy of who can and cannot speak to the media. If the wrong person grants an interview, she just might be fired.

But at the core of community organizing is the mission of developing leaders from affected communities who can speak for themselves, and so the question of who speaks to the media becomes more complicated. An organization that purports to be developing leaders and empowering communities through organizing but channels all media contact through an executive director is doing something wrong. It's missing out on a chance at leadership development and is falling into an advocacy role that forces those directly affected to sit on the sidelines and have others speak for them.

Some organizing groups have a clear policy that allows only members to speak to the media. Other organizations have a more flexible approach: on some issues, the staff weighs in, often when a reporter is calling just for a quick quote on a topic, but on days when an action is taking place, the members themselves do most of the talking. But it is always suspicious to see "organizing" groups mentioned in the media with only one or two officially designated spokespeople who happen to be on staff and are not personally impacted by the issue.

Insisting on the importance of affected members speaking directly to the media also means that there needs to be training. In preparing for an action, organizers should plan out the logistics of the event with their leaders and decide on what message they want to communicate so they are not led off-topic by the questions of reporters. Although reporters may speak at great length to members on the day of an event, they usually have to tell your story in just a few words, so it helps to stay relentlessly on-message. Training in media communication can include role-playing, with one member acting as the spokesperson and another as a combative and unsympathetic reporter.

TELLING A STORY WITH VISUAL AIDS

During one campaign, PACC was working with a coalition of housing organizations to pass code enforcement legislation that would give tenants more power to petition for comprehensive building inspections by the City. Even though we were finding many City councilmembers who supported the bill, the Department of Housing was steadfastly against it. The coalition decided to hold a march from the steps of City Hall to the Department of Housing headquarters; we brainstormed about a visual aid, and someone came up with constructing a "Wall of Shame." The "wall" turned into a fifty-foot-long section of heavy canvas, with blown-up photos of apartments from around the city that were in disastrous condition. Contrasted with the shiny headquarters of the housing agency, the wall would provide a beautiful juxtaposition and frame our issue effectively.

The media absolutely ate it up. When our advisory went out, reporters began calling immediately, and the item that they all first mentioned was the "Wall of Shame." How big was it going to be? What buildings were going to be on it? Who was going to be carrying it? On the day of the event many media representatives showed up, and though they all ended up filing stories that included details about the actual legislation and what it would do, this was not the primary draw. The draw was the wall itself and the title we had given the wall, which dramatized the urgent need for the City to do something in response to such horrendous conditions. From the many press releases they received that day, reporters picked ours; they decided that a group of tenants carrying a wall of shame directly to the headquarters of the housing agency was newsworthy.

Finding a Framework That Resonates

There is much new emphasis in organizing circles around framing issues and "messaging," terms adopted from the public relations industry. This development reflects the ongoing sophistication of the organizing craft, and it is critically important to think through ways to communicate ideas so that they resonate with the public, are easily understood, and play on some deeply held values.

A wonderful illustration of this potential occurred in a victorious series of campaigns run by Make the Road by Walking. In the Brooklyn neighborhood of Bushwick, many Spanish-speaking residents were finding themselves in situations where a lack of translators had serious negative repercussions. In the welfare offices and emergency rooms of hospitals, the inability to communicate could have disastrous consequences for the poor and working-class members of Make the Road—from being incorrectly denied Food Stamps to, in the most drastic possible scenario, serious injury or death due to incorrect medical diagnosis.

After surveying hundreds of people at welfare offices, Make the Road issued a report in 1999 highlighting the lack of translation services. "Originally we were framing it as a new immigrant issue," says codirector Andrew Friedman. "But some of our members were Puerto Rican, and they didn't see themselves as immigrants." In addition, as the organizing on the ground continued and the scope of the problem grew, Make the Road began thinking about crafting citywide legislation that would require translation services at all offices of the City's Human Resources Administration (HRA). It became clear that they were going to need strong support from the City Council's Black, Latino, and Asian Caucus, which was made up primarily of African-Americans.

"That helped us to rethink it as a civil rights issue," explains Friedman. With 25 percent of New Yorkers lacking English proficiency, not providing them with the means to communicate was discrimination based on national origin. Make the Road filed several civil rights complaints against hospitals with the office of the attorney general, which were substantiated and led to settlements and corrective action. Then, in 2003, Make the Road led a coalition that eventually passed the Equal Access to Health and Human Services Act. The legislation mandated translation and interpretation services at all HRA offices for services such as food stamps, Medicaid, and public assistance applications. They followed this up with several successful campaigns against hospitals for a lack of translation services and signage and then moved on to the problem of translation services for parents with children in school, leading Mayor Bloomberg to issue new regulations requiring a dramatic expansion of language-assistance services at New York City schools.

The language of civil rights and the power of the civil rights law transformed what might have been seen as an issue affecting only a few new arrivals into a campaign that resonated with many. "It was a strategic decision," says Friedman. "It also helped us because we didn't want to seem like we were focusing unfairly on the welfare caseworkers, who are members of DC37 [a strong labor union with primarily African-American members]. We wanted to be able to talk about it in a way so that the union and their members could empathize."

It needs to be remembered, however, that the emphasis on smartly framing our issues doesn't mean anything by itself. Complementing Make the Road's effective use of the civil rights framework was the group's dedicated, laborious, day-to-day organizing. Indeed, when organizers needed to mobilize residents to demonstrate the strength of their constituency, they did so in large numbers. They had a campaign with a specific goal, engaged in the behind-the-scenes work of organizing, and were able to talk about their work in ways that resonated deeply with the public and politicians.

BECOMING AN INVESTIGATIVE REPORTER

There are many times when organizers actually do all the grunt work of a reporter just to make sure that the press figures out that their story is worthy of coverage. Ever read a story that starts with, "Our newspaper has learned that . . ."? Wonder where it learned that? Often, when the issue has something to do with poverty or race or social justice generally, an organizer called up a reporter at the newspaper and *told* him. It's that simple.

I was once working in a large building in Crown Heights whose roof had been partially destroyed by a fire. After many months of waiting for repairs, the landlord still hadn't done a thing, and leaks were cascading through many of the apartments after each new rainfall.

Sifting through ownership documents, I found an address for the landlord. Looking up the address on Google Maps—the Internet makes some things just too easy—I could see that it was a large mansion in New Jersey, complete with a pool and perfectly landscaped lawn, and further research told me that it had been purchased for $1.3 million. I called up a contact at the *Daily News* and spoon-fed him the story, e-mailing photos of the destroyed apartments, a list of the open violations, phone numbers of the tenant leaders who had agreed to speak to the media, and address, description, and purchase information of the landlord's home, along with his home and work phone numbers. A few days later the paper ran the story, titled "Slumlord of the Manor," complete with a large photograph of the landlord's mansion. Not long after, the roof was repaired. The more information you can uncover, the better your chances of getting the media's attention. Sometimes, you've got to do the job for them.

How to Write Effective Press Releases and Media Advisories

Press releases and media advisories are announcements of an event that will occur. Advisories usually go out a few days before an event and are written in the future tense, while releases are sent out the morning of the event and are written in the past tense.

The goal of advisories and releases is to grab the attention of editorial desks and clearly illustrate the potential of the event. Though the substance behind the event is important, equally important is the ability to capture the issue dramatically through visuals and crisp details. Organizers shouldn't try to write a thesis on the issue or fill it with too many facts that deaden the impact of the overall message. Below is an actual advisory that PACC wrote for the "People's Housing Unit" action:

Media Advisory

Housing Court Refuses to Help Immigrant Families in Hazardous Building, So Tenants Create "People's Housing Unit," Don Code Enforcement Outfits, and Conduct Inspections of Homes to Deliver to Judge

Event: Brooklyn tenants of 230 Skillman and community activists come together to create grassroots housing inspection team, dress up in inspector outfits, and catalogue serious violations after Housing Court says they're too busy to help. "People's Housing Unit" members to take media representatives through a building inspection that highlights the violations, which includes peeling lead paint, gaping holes in the ceiling, a burst cold-water pipe on the first floor, faulty electric wiring, and an infestation of rats and cockroaches.

Date: Sunday February 3, 12 noon
Place: 230 Skillman Street in Bedford-Stuyvesant, Brooklyn
(between Dekalb & Willoughby)
Contact: Gabriel Thompson, PACC; (work) xxx-xxx-xxxx; (cell) xxx-xxx-xxxx

Otilia, a tenant of 230 Skillman, recently heard a loud crash and rushed into the room to find her ten-year-old daughter unconscious. A huge chunk of the ceiling had collapsed onto her child while she was working at the computer. When she and other tenants complained to the landlord about the conditions, nothing happened.

Finally, after months of struggling to get the landlord to fix the many violations—with no success—the tenants decided to take legal action. Accompanied by PACC, the tenants of 230 Skillman Street traveled to Brooklyn's Housing Court to file a lawsuit against their landlord for a lack of cold water (the tap only runs scalding), collapsing walls, and numerous other hazards.

After residents pooled their money to file the complaint, however, housing court representatives told the residents that they would be unable to inspect the building before the court date—even though there are many emergency conditions—because they didn't have enough building inspectors.

In response, the tenants and activists have created their own "People's Housing Unit" division—complete with jumpsuits and inspection forms—and will be going from apartment to apartment to record all of the violations for housing court. These violations will then be presented directly to the judge at the next court date on February 5.

The tenants of 230 Skillman and PACC are calling upon the City Council to increase funding to the city's code enforcement division, and for City Council to pass Intro 400a, a bill that would strengthen HPD's code enforcement division.

Your coverage is welcome.
Pratt Area Community Council
201 Dekalb Avenue, Brooklyn, NY 11205.
718-522-2613; fax 718-522-2604

WHY THE ADVISORY WORKS

Like all good advisories, the event is concisely summarized in the title. An assignment desk editor can quickly see that an injustice is occurring ("hazardous housing"), blame is being laid at the feet of a housing court that "refuses to help" (good versus evil), and the tenants are fighting back in a creative way. For television cameras and newspaper photographers, the violations listed also sound like they'll make for compelling images—as will a group of tenants wearing mock inspection outfits and taking on the shirked responsibility of the City by inspecting the building.

Notice, too, the mention of immigrant families. In towns and cities with sizable immigrant populations, an organizer should be mindful of tailoring her pitch to the ethnic media. For Spanish-language channels and newspapers, it is imperative to mention that the residents of the building are Latino immigrants: when we sent the above advisory to them, I added "Mexican" immigrants in the title. If there had been a Jamaican immigrant in the building, I would have edited another release focusing on this individual and sent it to the Caribbean press.

I also usually try to write advisories and releases that start with a dramatic first sentence that grabs people's attention. In this case, the lead was easy, since the collapsing ceiling was an obvious choice. The next few paragraphs outline the story, and the final sentence mentions the proposed legislation, which tenants made sure to mention to the media on the day of the event.

For events that involve compelling images, I try to have a few digital photos of the conditions that I can e-mail to the outlets to demonstrate that this will make a good story. In New York City, I often played a sick game with reporters: they would call up and say something like: "Well, how bad are the conditions that you're talking about? Am I going to be totally disgusted?" Sending a photo or two usually puts their mind at ease and guarantees they'll be at the action.

PITCHING THE ACTION

After sending out the media advisory, organizers should follow up with phone calls to make sure the outlet received the info and to outline briefly the potential drama of the event. It is also important to mention that people actually affected by the issue are going to be participating and will be available for interviews. With so many faxes and e-mails coming across the assignment desk, sometimes an effective pitch makes all the difference. Below are two examples of pitching an event to a reporter, again using the example of the People's Housing Unit.

> **Pitch Number 1:** I'm calling to let you know about a protest we're having in a building that has terrible conditions. The landlord hasn't been making repairs and the city won't inspect the building, so we're going to be giving a tour of the problems for the media. The tenants are really fed up and don't know what else to do, and we'd love it if you could be there.

> **Pitch Number 2:** I'm calling to let you know about an outrageous case in Brooklyn, where the city is refusing to fix a building that is virtually collapsing. Recently a chunk of the ceiling fell down and knocked out one of the tenant's children, and there are peeling lead paint and huge holes in the ceilings throughout, with rats and roaches scurrying about. The tenants sued the landlord in housing court, but the court said they don't have enough inspectors to come out to look at this emergency. The tenants have decided to form a guerrilla inspection team, called the "People's Housing Unit," and will be wearing inspector outfits and granting a tour of the building for the media. Since the city is refusing to help, the desperate tenants are taking matters into their own hand and hoping that your coverage will help them, and we'd love it if you could be there to hear their story.

Imagine, for a moment, the thought processes of the person at the assignment desk when receiving these two pitches. In pitch number 1, she hears that there will be a tour of a building in terrible condition. In New York City, this could describe thousands of buildings. That's not so unusual, is it? Hmm, maybe if it's a slow news day. . . . The same person hearing pitch number 2, however, has been given enough information to understand that this building has become a living hell (which is how one reporter characterized it in his piece). That a child was knocked out makes it that much more compelling, as does the fact that housing court has allegedly refused to take action. Nearly every local news station now seems to have its own "problem-solving" division, where a crusading reporter gets results when corporations or agencies don't do their jobs. The final line—"hoping that your coverage will help them"—plays on this trend.

One final note: don't spend lots of time introducing yourself and making small talk. Reporters and assignment desk editors are usually strapped for time, and the quicker you can make your case, the better.

DEVELOPING RELATIONSHIPS WITH REPORTERS

In many ways, reporters are similar to organizers. Reporters are always on the lookout for ways to dramatize issues, and some reporters cover specific beats, such as education or housing. Reporters want to break a story; organizers want to move an issue: It's a relationship that can be mutually beneficial.

When you have an event, keep track of who comes and what gets published. File away the information and remember to share potential stories with friendly contacts. Remember, if you pass along information to a reporter that turns into a good story, they'll remember you. This isn't always in the form of: "We're publishing a report and we wanted to give it to you first"; these are often more informal ideas, trends that might pan out, with a little digging, into a decent story. I would send an e-mail or give a quick call to a friendly journalist whenever I saw an issue that seemed promising. Reporters' days are often spent scavenging for leads, and in a certain sense they owe you for the tip. The more often you're able to hand over a good story, the more likely the reporter will be to show up at the next event.

That means, however, that you've got to be judicious with some of your contacts and not try to pitch everything to everybody. In Brooklyn, a slumlord story, complete with images of atrocious housing conditions, might interest the local television news or the *New York Post*. It probably won't, however, intrigue the *New York Times* unless it is somehow indicative of a trend or related to a policy failure. Know what stories certain outlets will be interested in covering—and pitch accordingly. Eventually, after a number of successful media events, reporters will come calling *you* to see if anything newsworthy is going on.

LOOK FOR PIGGYBACKING STORIES AND HISTORICAL TIE-INS

As you're organizing, keep track of national stories that might grant you a larger platform in pushing your work. If an item is making headlines and there's a way to tie that larger news story into local developments, getting into the news becomes a great deal easier.

Among other activities in Brooklyn, the Fifth Avenue Committee (FAC) organizes immigrant workers, mostly from Mexico. One day a number of grocery store janitors came in complaining about unpaid wages. As an afterthought, one of them mentioned that besides being owed money, the supervisor kept the doors of the store locked from the outside during the overnight cleanup shift. Supposedly to prevent theft, this meant that during their shifts the workers had no way to exit in the case of an emergency, such as a store fire.

Artemio Guerra, organizing director at FAC, immediately

understood the potential. "A light went off right away," he told me. "I knew this could become a big story." The *New York Times* had recently published a series of articles looking at complaints against Walmart, written by their labor correspondent, Steven Greenhouse. One of the complaints was that Walmart locked janitorial workers in overnight.

Guerra used the Walmart hook and sent out a press advisory to announce a protest: "A Walmart Scam Going on in Brooklyn?" The advisory, placing the local practice within a larger context, elicited many media inquiries, including interest from Greenhouse. Greenhouse would go on to write three articles, traveling to grocery stores unannounced and indeed finding locks on the supermarket doors, with workers stuck inside. FAC continued organizing and, with MFY Legal Services, also filed a lawsuit against a particularly irresponsible supermarket owner, serving the papers on the anniversary of the notorious Triangle Shirtwaist fire of 1911.

With the media coverage leading to sustained outrage, new legislation was passed in the City Council levying hefty fines on stores that engaged in the practice. On its own, the story had a lot going for it—exploited immigrant workers essentially imprisoned overnight. But also key to the campaign was an awareness of the different ways to highlight the problem, exemplified by FAC's ability to frame the issue within the context of Walmart's practices and the Triangle fire.

FINAL THOUGHT ON MEDIA:
Does Your Issue Really Need Another Press Conference?

I hate press conferences. When the weather is hot or cold, they suck. When the weather is pleasant, they're boring. When no press shows, they're absolutely pointless.

Unless there is especially enticing information being released, like our lead report described in the previous chapter, press conferences can be a drag. At press conferences, the people without a speaking role usually end up gathered well behind the podium, unable to hear what is going on, and forced simply to stand around and periodically break out into applause. For organizing groups, press conferences can sap the morale of members, who travel to the location and do little more than hold up a banner and then head home.

It's hard to find a press conference that wouldn't have been more effective as an action. Actions generally solicit more reporter interest and are much more enjoyable for members. If you have a report to release, make it into an action. For example, if the report criticizes the welfare department, far better than a press conference is to hold a rally in front of the main welfare office, speak to the press, and then have a group of leaders enter the building and attempt to deliver a special copy for the commissioner (perhaps along with a demand to meet to discuss the findings). That way, even if zero press representatives show up, you've accomplished something. The same goes for presenting petitions or postcards or any other sort of quantitative data: turn it into an action. Move your campaign.

During protracted campaigns, the temptation can be to call a press conference whenever something new surfaces. During our lead-paint organizing, the coalition spent several years battling the City Council, and by the end we were holding far too many conferences. For a while, the conferences were well attended, but at a certain point the number of reporters coming to record our events on the steps of City Hall dropped off dramatically. When we become predictable, the press loses interest. It's imperative to remain creative, to think of new ways to highlight the issue. And as organizers, we should never forget that some of the best ideas come from the members.

Chapter 7

HISTORY IS POWER:
Why Organizers Should Study Dead People

> *The long memory is the most radical idea in America.*
> —Clara Sparks

In the title of his classic work, the historian Edward Hawlett Carr posed the question *What Is History?* To nail down a definition of history is a treacherous and ultimately impossible task. History has different meanings for different people. At one end of the spectrum is the use of history as nothing more than a game of recalling past facts for entertainment, an effective whittling away of empty hours. For others, the study of history takes on more depth, helping people understand their cultural heritage and reclaim a pride that may have been stifled. For certain Americans, history is, for all practical purposes, dead. Sucked in by a culture that is increasingly ruled by "a tyranny of the present," to use the phrase of John Keane, a consciousness about things past has simply eroded.[1] A story blares across newspaper headlines and television channels for a few days and then drops forever down Orwell's memory hole. Hence when a new challenge confronts people, they are forced to scramble around with no historical compass to guide them, a situation that is naturally exploited by those with power seeking less-than-honorable ends.

In high school I became familiar with the study of history, which I greeted with a heavy dose of rebellion. My first reaction to the boring high school version of history was the familiar "Why study dead people?" query. I doubt I was looking to achieve a larger goal than instructor agitation, and in this project I was wildly successful. Teachers became easily exasperated, endlessly stammering an identical mantra: "Those who don't learn from history are bound to repeat it. . . . Those who don't . . . learn repeat . . . don't . . . history. . . . " Their jabber eventually sunk in, but with a peculiar selectivity—*don't learn history* became my new motto. If I was going to be coerced into spending an hour each day regurgitating facts not of my choosing, than the least I could do was to make sure they didn't find a resting spot in my head for the long haul. In this, too, I achieved my goal.

Then came college: a flurry of inspiring professors and subjects (the women's suffrage movement, the struggle for civil rights, the mobilization against the Vietnam War), a summer spent organizing in the labor movement and being steeped in labor history, a few trips to Latin America, and bam!—history had come to life.

But I never found myself drawn to this study in fear of repeating the past. In fact, I could never quite get an idea of *why* I devoured books of radical history with such vigor, aside from the inherently interesting stories they contained. Was it for simple inspiration, a need to put a brighter shine on my presently boring existence, some sick desire to know all kinds of esoteric facts? I eventually concluded that it was a combination of the above and left it at that.

But when I came to Brooklyn and became more and more engrossed in organizing, I also found myself relying increasingly on the use of history in ways I never could have imagined while in college. I had become accustomed to history as inspiration, but in the antiseptic confines of classrooms and lecture halls. I had experienced the joy of discovering new truths, but in the solitude of my safe apartment with unfamiliar books. And I had learned about hard-fought victories, but as a spectator, not as a participant.

My experiences as an organizer in Brooklyn have shed new light for me on the usefulness of history. History holds a special meaning for community organizers and all others committed to working within movements for social justice. History yields no easy answers, no formulas for success, no guarantees of victory. It does, however, demonstrate that the determination of heroic yet "ordinary" people has achieved whatever progress our country has made, and these moments of triumph can be relived, reflected upon, and converted into fuel for present-day efforts. As Howard Zinn writes: "History cannot provide confirmation that something better is inevitable; but it can uncover evidence that it is conceivable."[2]

As an organizer I relied on history in many ways, which I use this chapter to explore. Taking history from the orderly classroom to the messy world of organizing led to some critical discoveries— about myself, about the possibilities for personal transformation through the use of history, about history redefining the context of our own actions, and about the ability of history to provide the most enduring antidepressant medication for organizers confronting seemingly impossible situations. Carr asked: what is history? For organizers, history is power.

PASSING THE BATON

During my second year in college, before arriving in Brooklyn, I attended an anniversary in Oakland of the veterans of the Abraham Lincoln Brigade. The brigade was a group of idealistic and militant Americans who traveled to Spain to defend the democratically elected Popular Front government—a coalition of liberals, trade unionists, socialists, anarchists, and communists—against a fascist rebellion. The Spanish Civil War began in July 1936, when a group of Spanish generals attempted a military coup, achieving partial success and eventually gaining critical support from Hitler and Mussolini in the war that ensued. While the U.S. government remained ostensibly neutral (while actually allowing U.S. corporations to supply the fascists with oil and other goods), twenty-eight hundred Americans—most with ties to the Community Party—volunteered to fight against the fascist aggression.*

In Oakland, veterans were celebrating the sixtieth anniversary of their return, and I jumped at the opportunity to meet some of the folks while they were still alive. During the dinner break, I introduced myself to a tallish man whose name tag identified him as a veteran. He was eager to discuss his experiences—as all the veterans seemed to be—and left me with words that still ring in my ears.

"My grandfather fought in the Civil War to free the slaves," he said. "When he was dying he told me it was the right thing to do, that he had no regrets." The veteran paused for a moment, caught up in the memory. "Then I fought in Spain," he continued. "I suppose I inherited his radical blood. Now I'm old and I'm pretty

---

* Those who returned from fighting in Spain—one out of three were killed in action—later enlisted to fight in World War II and were discriminated against by the U.S. government, which labeled brigade members "premature antifascists" (as if it's ever premature to resist fascism).

much through fighting. So I'm passing it along to you; here's the baton." He pretended to drop a baton in my hand, as if we were running a relay, and smiled at his pantomime.

I remember the moment, standing there in a room full of senior-citizen activists, wishing I could preserve his statement on tape. He smiled again at nothing in particular and then nodded and ambled over to the food table to grab a tuna fish sandwich.

The veteran's phrase has stayed with me; passing the baton has become a favorite metaphor for the power and purpose of historical study. One can envision different races occurring simultaneously around the world. Some are racing for money and increased privilege, grabbing the baton (and an incredible lead) from wealthy parents and steaming full speed ahead. Some are instead racing for military hegemony, and some for political gain. Some, too, like this veteran of the Spanish Civil War, are racing for the creation of a world based on more humane values. The lives we choose to live will determine which baton we shall carry to our own finish line, and I hope we, too, can find younger generations to carry on the struggle before we expire.

Some, like myself, are lucky enough to have someone present us with an inspiring baton early on. Others have ugly batons forced into their hands, without knowledge of alternative batons they could carry. The study of history, then, can help dig up unknown and inspiring batons from the past. It can also help us connect to individuals and movements greater than ourselves and remind us that the track we are running on is sacred.

FROM LANDLORD TO LIBERATOR

I spent a lot of my time organizing in the neighborhood of Northwest Bedford-Stuyvesant, which was bursting with low-income Hasidic Jews, recently arrived Mexican immigrants and more established Latinos, and longtime African-American residents. Although all parties share a same basic need—safe and affordable

housing—racial tensions are predictably high and manifest themselves in various ways. Mexican tenants often no longer call people
landlords, instead referring to "*los judíos*"—the Jews. Mythical stories circulate in bars and restaurants about Jewish landlords who
burn down entire buildings with tenants inside, and many of these
sentiments are given further ammunition by reactionary neighborhood preachers.

Nearly all of the apartments in this neighborhood are in disre-
pair. During the winter months it seemed that every day another
family was calling to complain about not having heat or hot water.
One mother came to a meeting and spoke about her five-year-old
daughter, who had caught pneumonia because their landlord had
shut off the heat in an attempt to "persuade" the tenants to leave.
Children were being poisoned by lead paint, cockroaches were
omnipresent, and ceilings were collapsing. It was a neighborhood
perfectly characterized by having, in the concise jargon of urban
planners, a crumbling housing stock.

One building in particular had a notoriously bad slumlord. It
was in such awful shape that when a crisis *wasn't* happening in the
building for a few weeks, I would stop by just to make sure the tenants' phone lines hadn't gone down. The tenants of the building
were either Latino or African-American, and the landlord—who
didn't live in the neighborhood—was a Hasidic Jew. I had come to
expect the many anti-Semitic comments from the tenants and had
mostly let them slide by without challenge, wanting first to gain
their acceptance as the new organizer. Still, I knew that I would
eventually need to make my views known: that the situation was
due to landlord greed and not some racial formula.

After a few months of working with the tenants, I decided that
it was time to try to begin a dialogue about the anti-Semitic comments. From the research I had done immediately after beginning
my work in Brooklyn, I knew that the tenant movement in the
United States had begun in the Lower East Side of Manhattan
during the Depression. I collected landlord statements from the

period, as well as demands made by the tenant rebels, who just so happened to be Jewish (and some of whom would likely go on to volunteer in the Abraham Lincoln Brigade).

It was at a tenant association meeting that I decided to breach the subject. I explained that the families being booted into the streets and fighting with the police back then were Jewish, and that they had suffered the same types of conditions as the very building we were meeting in, if not worse.

"The Jews?" asked Esmerelda, a Guatemalan who had lived on the second floor for fifteen years. "These Jews here aren't like that."

"They would organize themselves into teams," I continued, ignoring her comment for the moment. "Back then the police would just come and take all the belongings out of a family's home and put them in the street. Landlords didn't even have to take tenants to court, just call up the cops and have 'em drag everything out. So Jewish tenants got together into teams and would go to buildings where people were being evicted. They'd just pick up the furniture and bring it back in—didn't even care if the cops were watching. So they'd get beaten a lot, but they also kept a lot of families from being evicted."

Sabrina, a woman from Costa Rica whom I hadn't heard say anything derogatory about Jews, whistled in amazement. "I tell you, I won't give up here—even if the landlord thinks he can evict me. We've got to fight and I'll keep going . . . but I don't know about those folks. I wouldn't want to get beat by cops. Ha!" she laughed. "Getting beat by cops, taking clothes and everything back in! That's what we need around here, a little more attitude like that."

"But here no Jew is doing that," Esmerelda interjected. "Our landlord isn't going to be standing up for us, get beat by cops or nothing."

"Well, why not?" I asked.

"Gabriel, he's a landlord. Why'd he be helping us when he's a landlord? It doesn't make sense. He just wants our money. That's all he cares about."

"Okay, so he's being a bad landlord," I conceded. "But look, what if he were a tenant here?"

The tenants all had a good laugh about this idea. "Here? That'll be the day," said Luz, a seventy-year-old tenant who had lived in the building more than forty years.

"He wouldn't live here like this," added Sabrina. "That's for sure. He'd probably complain more than us, get everything fixed up, since he's not used to living like this. He'd probably complain even more than me!" She was laughing now at the thought.

"No one complains more than you!" shouted Esmerelda. "*Nadie!*"

After everyone had commented about the determination of Sabrina to document each and every code violation, I finished by being as explicit as possible about my feelings.

"The reason I wanted to have this meeting is because I disagree with the idea that the problem is the Jews. I don't think that your landlord is bad because he is Jewish. I think he's bad because he is acting like a landlord, harassing you and not repairing things. And some of us might turn into bad people, too, if we started owning lots of property—I've seen white, black, Puerto Rican landlords that all were terrible.

"I know that you have lived here much longer than me. But I'm just telling you what I think. Where I'm from, in California, people say the same things about Mexicans—that they're all lazy, they don't know how to work. You've heard the same shit. I think it's the same when people say Jews are all bad. Just look at what the Jews were doing in this City, fighting cops to keep families from being evicted! I don't know anyone that has guts like that today. I know I don't."

This last sentence ended the meeting. The results weren't magical; no one instantly leapt up with joy at the new facts being presented, ready to embrace every Jew on the street. Tenants still continued to make comments about Jewish landlords, if only remembering to do so under their breath, safely out of earshot.

But it did, I certainly hope, help remind the tenants what dynamic was keeping them in squalid conditions, and it showed them that complaints identical to their own had been made in the past by those they identified as the "enemy," placing the blame squarely on the shoulders of abusive landlords—regardless of their background. A retelling of history had allowed an interpretation of the problem different from the usual one among the tenants, and it is from such limited breathing room that profound transformations must always begin.

HISTORY AS POLITICAL EDUCATION

As I argue in Chapter 4, without an emphasis on political education, one can easily find oneself developing leaders whose agenda is far from progressive. To take the example of the tenants angry with their Jewish landlord—well, they were certainly motivated and engaged. They trusted me and would come out for meetings and take part in direct actions. They were pissed off about having to live in horrible conditions and wanted to do something about it. The tenants obviously didn't harbor any elaborate ideology against Jews; their opinions were informed only by their immediate experiences. It would be easy to ignore their prejudices when they surfaced and avoid the risk of alienating engaged members. Why bother trying to tackle their knee-jerk anti-Semitism?

As I point out above, organizers need to tackle thorny issues with their members and not turn a blind eye in hopes of glossing over a conflict. Community organizers with some knowledge of history can prod their members by using examples as means to inspire, compare, or better understand present difficulties. Had I told the tenants with the Jewish landlord, "Hey, you shouldn't dislike Jews, cause I think some are fine people," it would have held no resonance. It would have been just one claim against many others, with no evidence to support it against their personal experiences with Jews (this one landlord). Instead I tried to ask what it was about landlords who owned many properties: Why did they seem to behave badly over the course of a hundred years? This critique leads to broad questions about society: Where do human rights and property rights collide? Which has more importance? Is shelter a speculative investment for people with money? A human right for everyone? Both? Have other people asked these questions? What kinds of answers did they come up with?

Debating these types of questions is what political education is all about. Often the "problem" identified in a community may just be the most visible manifestation of a larger issue—just as when tenants focused their criticism on their Jewish landlord and not on, for instance, the real estate interests or cowardly politicians that allowed the rights of tenants to be gradually worn down. Relying on history for guidance and as a means to explore issues with more depth enables organizers and community members to start thinking outside the box, asking more fundamental questions about what is wrong, and positing solutions that go to the core of the issue.

History can also become a critical aspect of political education through the study of periods of social change and how such movements were able to succeed. If people discover that such glorious events actually happened the old-fashioned way—through hope and hard work—then suddenly we've got all the qualifications to do the same.

WHY THE FARMWORKERS WENT OUT ON STRIKE

Alfredo deAvila is a senior program associate at the Applied Research Center and previously worked for many years as a senior trainer with the Center for Third World Organizing (CTWO), both based in Oakland, California. A high school dropout, he began organizing in Texas, spending many years with the farmworkers during the 1960s.

"Since the farmworker movement has been so glorified, people forget that a lot of workers walked out on strike, got black-listed, and never got jobs again," deAvila explained. "Some of them paid an extremely heavy price for the stuff they did. I knew people that got hurt, I knew people that were killed in the course of different strikes."

The counterattacks that the farmworkers in Texas suffered were extensive, as deAvila told me: "Sometimes when we had strikes the Texas Rangers came in, kicked the shit out of us, had people arrested all over the goddamn place, threatened to kill union members, sent people to jail on bullshit trumped up charges." He paused to catch his breath. "Then they'd tie up a hundred thousand dollars in cash bonds, get court injunctions that said we couldn't stand two people on the damn street corner without breaking some law or another."

I asked Alfredo how they got anyone to walk off the fields in that type of environment, with such immediate and drastic consequences to striking. He answered:

> That's a good question. You can always sit there and say: "Shit, if we hadn't started it maybe none of our people would have been killed. If we hadn't started it nobody would have lost their jobs, nobody would have lost their homes." But people did make those sacrifices, and they did so because they were thinking about a bigger picture beyond their own problems. We tried to sell a bigger picture than just the battle around wages in the fields. I tell folks that I pulled more farmworkers out on strike not because of what we could win immediately, but because they wanted to stop the discrimination and racism that existed in the fields.
>
> They were tired of being used and being exploited, tired of the bosses looking down on them simply because they were Latinos. They had no drinking water, no rest

breaks, were being treated like animals instead of human beings. And the issue that caused folks to strike was to stop that whole damn thing. Not about the fact that we can make a dollar-fifty more on wages, not even always that we could stop the discrimination right away. Farmworkers went out on strike so that their children and their grandchildren wouldn't have to go through the same shit that they went through, and their fathers before them. And I tell people that's why I got more farmworkers to strike, to take such a risk.

It was a shared history—a history that crossed generations, united families, solidified communities. "Farmworkers understood their history, because their parents had worked in the fields, too," deAvila continued. "This history that we all shared allowed us to talk about the farmworker, to appeal to people to say it's time to end this exploitation, to end this history of a people that feed the nation but who can't feed their own families."

Another challenge to organizing farmworkers was the cyclical nature of the work. Alfredo laughed loudly, remembering his exploits:

You know, we were asking them to stop working at the only time of the year when there was work. Great, you've been sitting around three months starving, and you had no money, the work is just starting, and some crazy son-of-a-bitch organizer comes and says, "Yo, let's not go to work now!" But many of them decided, even with all the repression, that they weren't going to work, because they wanted to leave a better world for their children. They knew the history of the farmworker, and they believed that they could change it—that they had to change it or else their children would have to suffer the same humiliations.

FROM TINA TO TINBA:

Organizing to Insert the "B"

As prime minister of Great Britain, Margaret Thatcher coined the term TINA: There Is No Alternative. It's a logical phrase for any despotic political leader to make; what power-hungry individual wouldn't want the ability to say what is and isn't possible in the world? TINA was meant to demoralize people who were dissatisfied with the present arrangement of things, to make sure that they understood that regardless of whatever hopes, dreams, and aspirations they carried in their hearts, it was pointless to attempt to change anything. There Is No Alternative.

Along a similar but gentler line of thinking, Francis Fukuyama's book *The End of History and the Last Man* argues that all political ideas have been exhausted and that the only remaining alternative is the model of capitalist democracy, which is best exemplified by the United States. Fukuyama's argument, which he has since smartly backed away from, was similar to Thatcher's TINA: for better or for worse, present-day realities exist only because all other plausible alternatives have failed. In the views of both Thatcher and the earlier Fukuyama, there is no longer any profound tension—deficient options for the way society can be organized have been tossed out, and we have arrived at *the way things are,* which is also, conveniently, how they should be.

Organizers, on the other hand, had better feel some serious tension—or they are in the wrong business. This tension, as Ed Chambers writes, is not necessarily negative:

> In today's culture, tension is a bad word, always quickly followed in advertising by "relief." The media teaches that tensions mean we're "stressed out" or "uptight" or "wound up"—all undesirable states calling for immediate medication, therapy, or exercise. But the tension

I'm naming here isn't a problem to be solved. It's the human condition. It's the gap that people who aren't completely lost in the culture of self-centeredness feel between the reality that surrounds them and their ideals.[3]

The tension is again between the world as it is and the world as it should be.

The powerful fear this tension and so must invent terms like TINA out of a sense of profound insecurity. The historian Harvey Kaye touches on this insecurity in a collection of essays entitled *Why Do Ruling Classes Fear History?* Ruling classes fear history for the same reason Margaret Thatcher coined and promoted TINA: in reality, there is nothing but alternatives. Organizers exist in part to provide the guidance and assistance to people that is needed to insert the "but," so that the possibilities for change come alive again.

Every predicament we find ourselves in today, from the corporate ownership of the media to the 40 million Americans without health insurance, can appear inevitable, the result of a natural evolution. However, when one starts digging into the past, events begin popping up demonstrating that thoughtful alternatives were presented to avoid such scenarios. The entire point of a phrase like TINA is to obfuscate this important truth. Nearly every time I've had the thought that perhaps I was simply being difficult regarding an issue—that I was too idealistic or demanding for the world— I've looked back in the history books and found that in the past thousands of people sacrificed and struggled for the same cause or for even more radical changes. I hope we can remember that people in this country fought (and died) for the eight-hour workday; they fought for the *four-hour workday*. There is nothing but alternatives: TINBA.

The insertion of this "but" is strengthened by organizers who are able to call up past events that show how much effort was necessary for the powerful to squash more humane and progressive alternatives and highlight times when ordinary people were able to create extraordinary change. People taught to believe that "it's just the way things are" can learn that in fact "the way things are" often changed because people just like themselves took action. When we transform TINA to TINBA, we recognize that the tension generated by acting on our best impulses opens up doors that seemed permanently locked, and in doing so we encourage others to follow our lead.

HISTORY AND THE COMMUNITY ORGANIZER

This chapter argues that history can be used by organizers to teach, inspire, agitate, and compare. In his book *Taking History to Heart,* James Green writes that "historical narratives can do more than redeem the memory of past struggles; they can help people think of themselves as historical figures with crucial moral and political choices to make, like those who came before them."[4] This is the greatest power of history for organizers and the communities they are organizing in: the ability to reinterpret our lives and the meaning of them. We are taught that history is made by the wealthy and fortunate in the corridors of power. We can learn that it is also made by the less powerful, in the streets and unpublicized meetings, by people who refuse to give up.

Following this line of thinking, one can begin to view the history of social movements as something akin to an eager army just waiting to be called up for active duty. Alone or with a few people, the world can be a very frightening and hostile place apparently inhospitable to radical social change. But by dredging up the memories and inspiration of hundreds of years of progressive struggle, one can envision oneself as part of this army—an army that has achieved very substantial gains in the face of great odds.

But history is not just instructive for movements—it is also necessary for the individual organizer, helping to sustain his or her efforts. For myself, history has become an antidepressant of sorts. I am not an optimist by nature; I am an optimist by effort. It takes effort to be a part of so many losing battles and to continue on without becoming profoundly bitter. It takes effort to see promise in a country where miniature dogs walk down Madison Avenue wearing fleece jackets while families shiver outside soup kitchens. It takes effort to hear empty rhetoric about "values" from privileged politicians who have never known poverty and then to turn off the television and continue to be confronted with people who must struggle for basic rights like health care and housing. And it takes effort not to retreat into the not-quite-happy but safely familiar cynicism and sarcasm that for me is never completely out of arm's reach.

The potential for creating progressive change can seem entirely hopeless when viewed in a contextless, ahistorical vacuum. And so our study of history—our effort—helps bind us to forces of greater inspiration, to persons who faced similar situations in the past and whose determination inspires awe. How could we possibly turn away from them—and what better way to honor the past accomplishments of our heroes than to use them in present struggles? We need to remember the people who came before us and we need to share them with others who have never heard of folks like Ella Baker or organizations like the Student Nonviolent Coordinating Committee. For we, too, are simple and we, too, will be forgotten by most history books—but we, too, can change the world.

Chapter 8

PREPARING FOR FRUSTRATION:
The Montgomery Bus Boycott You Never Knew

What you do may seem insignificant, but it is most important that you do it.
—Mohandas Gandhi

Why do so many organizers leave the field so quickly? The simplest answer is that they've been sold a bill of goods that doesn't deliver. Some might be drawn to the promise of organizing after seeing inspirational documentaries that highlight the drama and overlook the drudgery. Others perhaps have taken part in exciting large-scale protests, showing up and making their voices heard for the day, and imagine that this is what a career in organization entails. The word itself, organize, is laden with notions of romance, of action and struggle and—at the end—victory.

What isn't so inspiring is the frustration that comes with

organizing, often surfacing most strongly early in the career of an organizer. One jumps into the field of organizing with all sorts of notions of what the work will be like, and when those notions don't always receive confirmation (and they won't), it can be dispiriting. During my first few months on the job, I was attempting to organize mostly Latino immigrants around poor housing conditions. I went out door knocking and didn't have much luck; many of the tenants frankly explained that I was wasting my time. Housing court wouldn't do anything, the City wouldn't do anything, everyone was afraid to take action because they didn't want to be deported.

"Why are you wasting time knocking on my door?" I only had to hear that twice before serious doubts began to creep in. Why *was* I knocking on their door? Who was I trying to fool?

Another tenant I remember laid out a similar complaint: the City doesn't care about fixing our apartments because to them we're just poor Mexicans. "What can you do about *that?*" the man snarled.

I explained that I had no special knowledge, that I was just an organizer who worked to bring people together so they could change the system. I've never spoken words that felt emptier. The tenant looked at me in disbelief, and walking away from his apartment, I had to agree. I had recently spent six weeks door knocking in a certain area, and after all the effort, what had I accomplished? I called a meeting, and only five people bothered to show up. Five people was barely a dinner party. Making matters worse, I knew that poor housing conditions were a common complaint—it was all people seemed to talk about. But when it came to moving them to become involved, I was failing miserably.

I had read books about organizing; I knew how this was supposed to work. Organizers go out into a community, knock on doors and talk to people, call a meeting, find out what the issues are, give the group some direction, et cetera, et cetera. Then the people come together and demand change in some capacity, and the world becomes a better place. Hadn't all my studies in history given me hope, after all?

THE DOCUMENTARIES THAT AREN'T MADE

Imagine watching a documentary about organizing that is, say, forty-eight hours long. You follow an organizer as he gets doors slammed in his face, as he stares blankly at a computer screen, as he comes home from work confused about what he's doing, as he sits anxiously in empty church basements waiting for people to begin filing in. Three boxes of pizza sit on a table, getting cold. The church janitor peeks in and wonders who all the food is for. "I'm hungry," he says. "Mind if I have a slice?" The organizer holds out for another half hour—still hoping that a dozen folks might just be running late—but eventually gives in, handing all three boxes to the man. The camera follows the organizer as he heads home. It's probably raining.

While it might lack cinematic quality, this documentary captures experiences that nearly every organizer has dealt with at one time or another. All these experiences are edited out—for good reason. They're not inherently interesting or compelling. There is no moral struggle against an obvious injustice. No chanting, no picketing, no tears (except perhaps in self-pity; not exactly inspiring). They would be boring, unremarkable, hard to sit through. But they would have one thing going for them, and that is accuracy.

EMBRACING FRUSTRATION

This chapter examines frustration. It is not meant to teach young organizers how they can avoid such feelings, which at times may briefly border on despair. Periodic feelings of frustration and despair are two inevitable and necessary building blocks for the creation of social movements, as long as they do not immobilize and overwhelm us. The world *can* be quite harsh and hard to change, and when we organize, we place ourselves right in the middle of this harshness.

Instead, I want to explore ways we can learn to live with and even embrace frustration, with the explicit understanding that every project in pursuit of justice will be difficult. By understanding the long-term effort that must go into every movement, we become better able to avoid burnout and accurately place our frustrations within a more realistic framework. If organizers don't come to grips with this framework, they will most certainly end up throwing in the towel early, disappointed that their work is not achieving the instant results that they had hoped for.

I begin this exploration by way of history, with a brief examination of the origins of the Montgomery Bus Boycott, which illustrates the behind-the-scenes work that went into the spectacular action that launched the civil rights movement (covered briefly in the Introduction). After reflecting on the lessons of the boycott, the issue of burnout is addressed, as well as the need to recognize that we are not perfect and that we must refuse to let our imperfection make us demoralized when we do not achieve everything that we have set out for ourselves. All this is to remind us that we can always awake to fight another day.

THE MONTGOMERY BUS BOYCOTT YOU NEVER KNEW

Not too long after the depressingly small meeting turnout, I came across a small gem of a book. Browsing in the local library, my eyes were drawn to *The Montgomery Bus Boycott and the Women Who Started It,* by Jo Ann Gibson Robinson. It was a thin book, wedged between the more recognizable *Autobiography of Malcolm X* and books on topics like the NAACP and Black Panthers. I was immediately intrigued by the title. Women had started the boycott? What I knew about the event was the little I could conjure up from high school: Martin Luther King Jr. had led it, and Rosa Parks had been the woman who triggered the boycott by refusing to get up from her seat on the bus. Perhaps this was what the author meant when she said that women had started the boycott. But what other women could she be talking about? I hadn't heard of any other famous women who had taken part in the boycott.

When I opened the book I was greeted by a photocopied letter dated May 21, 1954, addressed to Montgomery's mayor, W. A. Gale. It read:

> *Dear Sir:*
>
> *The Women's Political Council is very grateful to you and the City Commissioners for the hearing you allowed our representatives during the month of March, 1954, when the "city-bus-fare-increase case" was being reviewed.*
>
> *There were several things the Council asked for:*
>
> *—A city law that would make it possible for Negroes to sit from back toward front, and whites from front toward back until all the seats are taken;*
>
> *—That Negroes not be asked or forced to pay fare at front and go to the rear of the bus to enter;*
>
> *—That buses stop at every corner in residential sections occupied by Negroes as they do in communities where whites reside.*
>
> *We're happy to report that buses have begun stopping at more corners now in some sections where Negroes live than previously. However, the same practices in seating and boarding the bus continue.*
>
> *Mayor Gayle, three-fourths of the riders of those public conveyances are Negroes. If Negroes did not patronize them, they could not possibly operate.*
>
> *There has been talk from twenty-five or more local organizations of planning a city-wide boycott of buses. . . .*
>
> *Please consider this plea, and if possible, act favorably upon it, for even now plans are being made to ride less, or not at all, on our buses. We do not want this.*
>
> *Respectfully yours,*
>
> *The Women's Political Council*
> *Jo Ann Robinson, President*[1]

If I was reading the document correctly, eighteen months before Rosa Parks refused to cede her seat, this letter was delivered to the mayor of Montgomery, warning of a possible boycott. My previous understanding of the boycott had been that it was a spontaneous affair, a mass uprising by people reacting to a glaring injustice. I had always thought of it as one of those "lucky" historical incidents, a movement that came about almost by accident.

But then how to explain this letter? It looked as though citizens in Montgomery, at least the ones behind this document, were organizing prior to most people's understanding of the beginning of the boycott—which leads to more questions. Who was this Jo Ann Robinson? And what about the organization of which she was president, the Women's Political Council? What role did they play in the boycott, this group that in 1954 was diplomatically threatening the mayor with a boycott? Most important, why hadn't I ever heard of any of this before?

It turned out that the organization that would go on to call the boycott, the Women's Political Council (WPC), was formed in 1946 by Dr. Mary Fair Burks, chairperson of the English department at Alabama State College in Montgomery. She had been born in Alabama, where many of the members would be drawn from. They were largely professional women, who had what Jo Ann Gibson Robinson called "woman power." In 1950 Robinson became the head of the organization, succeeding Burks. Up until the boycott, the WPC worked primarily on registering black citizens to vote, working with youth, and acting on various complaints from the community. By 1955 the WPC had three chapters, each with roughly a hundred members. These three groups were organized according to geography, allowing a communications system to operate throughout the city of Montgomery, which would prove critical for the future success of the boycott.

It was December 1, 1955, a Thursday, when Rosa Parks decided she would not relinquish her seat to a white man. Rosa Parks, now having reached virtual sainthood in the United States, was at the time an ordinary woman with an extraordinary political consciousness. She was a longtime NAACP activist, had attended organizing classes at the Highlander Folk School, and though she was obviously "tired" of making room for white folks, she had clearly contemplated the potential consequences of such a refusal.

Word of her arrest spread rapidly through the African-American community of Montgomery; veteran NAACP leader E. D. Nixon, along with white attorney Clifford Durr, paid Parks's bond. For Robinson and the WPC, the perfect opportunity for a boycott had arrived. Parks's trial on December 5 was the natural occasion to begin the protest. In preparation for a boycott, the WPC had already developed, prior to the arrest of Parks, an infrastructure for the distribution of thousands of notices. WPC members had been waiting for the right moment to arrive; with Parks, they figured their patience had finally paid off. As Robinson writes:

> I sat down and quickly drafted a message and then called a good friend and colleague, John Cannon, chairman of the business department at the college, who had access to the college's mimeograph equipment. When I told him that the WPC was staging a boycott and needed to run off the notices, he told me that he too had suffered embarrassment on the city buses. Like myself, he had been hurt and angry. He said that he would happily assist me. Along with two of my most trusted senior students, we quickly agreed to meet almost immediately, in the middle of the night, at the college's duplicating room. We were able to get three messages to a page, greatly reducing the number of pages that had to be mimeographed in order to produce the tens of thousands of leaflets we knew would be needed. By 4 AM Friday, the sheets had been duplicated, cut in thirds, and bundled.[2]

The notices that had been produced into the early hours of the morning announced the boycott in uncompromising language:

> *Another Negro woman has been arrested and thrown in*
> *jail because she refused to get up out of her seat on the bus*
> *for a white person to sit down. . . . Three-fourths of the*
> *riders are Negroes, yet we are arrested, or have to stand over*
> *empty seats. . . . We are, therefore, asking every Negro to stay*
> *off the buses Monday in protest of the arrest and trial.*[3]

On that afternoon, the WPC and other helpers distributed the leaflets. Within hours most African-Americans in the city either had a copy of the leaflet in hand or had heard the information relayed to them through word of mouth. It also happened that many of Montgomery's black clergy were meeting at the Hilliard Chapel A.M.E. Zion Church that morning, and care was made to drop off a number of flyers for them. The members present who belonged to the city's congregations threw their weight behind the boycott immediately, without waiting for approval from their ministers. E. D. Nixon understood the time was ripe for change. He gathered together important community members, including King, to decide on the appropriate actions. The ministers supported the idea of a boycott but did not want to come out publicly to endorse it, fearful of a white backlash. This hesitancy did not sit well with Nixon:

> *"What the hell you talkin' about?" he demanded. "How*
> *you gonna have a mass meeting, gonna boycott a city bus*
> *line without the White folks knowing it?" Nixon was*
> *merciless. He told them: "You guys have went around*
> *here and lived off these poor washerwomen all your lives*
> *and ain't never done nothing for 'em, you talkin' about*
> *you don't want the White folks to know it." He then*
> *threatened to tell the community that the boycott would*
> *be called off because the ministers were "too scared."*[4]

Nixon's scolding was effective; the ministers would publicly support the boycott. The Montgomery Improvement Association

(MIA) was created, and Nixon convinced King to accept the role of president of the organization.

On December 5, the endurance and organization of the WPC paid off. No African-Americans were seen riding the Montgomery buses. As the boycott developed, it depended on the infrastructure developed by the black community to carry on. Alternate modes of transportation were found, lines of communication were created, and funding started to flow in from outside organizations. Montgomery quickly became national news, and seemingly overnight King became known to millions around the country as the spokesperson for what was being called the civil rights movement.

The rest, as they say, is history. What gets forgotten, however, is how history itself was made. It was the WPC that had planned the boycott in advance and had forced the citizens and ministers to a decision by printing and distributing the leaflets. Without the already existing activist organizations, the boycott could have easily been a dismal and embarrassing failure, much as King's experience in Chicago would prove to be for the movement years later, when he mounted a failed campaign to combat housing discrimination without a significant indigenous base already established. In Montgomery, however, local citizens had been working together for years without white publicity. This work, sustained without any guarantee of future success, allowed for the creation and eventual success of the boycott and in doing so, handed the national microphone to King for the first time.

As I learned more about the Montgomery Bus Boycott, I realized that the event had much to teach about community organizing. From 1946 to 1955 the WPC was organizing with very little fanfare. The real work of organizing, largely invisible to the public eye, was the creation of relationships between ordinary citizens of Montgomery. Their boycott catapulted King to the position of national spokesperson for African-Americans and saw the eventual victory against the segregated busing system of Montgomery.

For many Americans, Rosa Parks symbolized the plight of

blacks in America, someone who had worked hard during her life and was simply "tired" of accepting the many injustices that came her way. But many of our popular conceptions of the boycott, though not incorrect in the narrowest sense, serve to confuse the reasons for its success. The rise of King was critical for the movement in general, but it does little to explain why the boycott achieved its goals and sheds no light on who called the boycott and took part in it. King himself understood the importance of the mass base in the victory of the bus boycott. In his book chronicling the event, he begins with an appropriate assessment:

> While the nature of this account causes me to make frequent use of the pronoun "I," in every important part of the story it should be "we." This is not a drama with only one actor. More precisely it is the chronicle of 50,000 Negroes who took to heart the principles of nonviolence, who learned to fight for their rights with the weapon of love, and who, in the process, acquired a new estimate of their own human worth.[5]

Sure, my first experiences organizing in Brooklyn weren't yielding quick gains, but organizing doesn't ever yield quick gains. After the initial "rush" from jumping into the world of social justice, I had hit a wall, disappointed that I hadn't caused an immediate splash. But who could tell what lay ahead? Who could have predicted that a small group of women in Montgomery would have initiated the first great protest to signal the beginning of revolutionary change for African-Americans?

THE FLYWHEEL EFFECT

The business writer Jim Collins, in his book *Good to Great,* makes a similar point about successful corporations, using the image of a flywheel to help explain their achievements. The flywheel, as Collins describes, is a massive metal disk weighing 5,000 pounds, and a company's metaphorical task is to get the flywheel moving somehow. The company goes to work, slowly at first, and as all the workers continue to push in the same direction, momentum begins to build. He is worth quoting at length:

> Then, at some point—breakthrough! The momentum of the thing kicks in in your favor, hurling the flywheel forward, turn after turn . . . whoosh! . . . its own heavy weight working for you. You're pushing no harder than during the first rotation, but the flywheel goes faster and faster. Each turn of the flywheel builds upon work done earlier, compounding your investment of effort. A thousand times faster, then ten thousand, then a hundred thousand. The huge heavy disk flies forward, with almost unstoppable momentum.
>
> Now suppose someone came along and asked, "What was the one big push that caused this thing to go so fast?"
>
> You wouldn't be able to answer; it's just a nonsensical question. Was it the first push? The second? The fifth? The hundredth? No! It was all of them added together in an overall accumulation of effort applied in a consistent direction. . . .
>
> No matter how dramatic the end result, the good-to-great transformations never happened in one fell swoop. There was no single defining action, no grand program, no one killer innovation, no solitary lucky break, no wrenching revolution. Good to great comes about by a cumulative process—step by step, action by action, decision by decision, turn by turn of the flywheel—that adds up to sustained and spectacular results.
>
> Yet to read media accounts of the companies, you might draw an entirely different conclusion. Often, the

*media does not cover a company until the flywheel is
already turning at a thousand rotations per minute.
This entirely skews our perception of how such transformations happen, making it seem as if they jumped right to
breakthrough as some sort of overnight metamorphosis.*[6]

The dynamic that Collins describes, of humble but steady
beginnings leading to spectacular results—and the popular mis-
conceptions of how that success was achieved nearly instantly—
provides a precise parallel to how a great social movement must
always begin. Like the Montgomery Bus Boycott and the civil
rights movement it ushered in, the flywheel was being pushed
slowly by citizens of Montgomery during years when the media
was largely unaware of their efforts. When the flywheel began to
pick up momentum, the country was stunned, leaving many to
wonder: "Where did that come from?" Organizers need to
remember that their efforts, which may frequently seem inconsequential, are critical, because only by continuing to push on the
flywheel do we keep alive the possibility for breakthrough.

ADDRESSING THE QUESTION OF BURNOUT

Keeping in mind concepts like the flywheel can help organizers
place their daily frustrations into a context that enables them to
avoid becoming easily discouraged. This is the long-range, historical orientation. Yet while acknowledging the need for a long-term
perspective, organizers must also guard against the occurrence of
ordinary short-term burnout.

All organizers (and, for that matter, all people who work) have to
deal with the problem of normal, run-of-the-mill burnout. Burnout
happens for a variety of reasons, but it is caused most frequently by
working too many hours for too long, expecting too much too soon,
and forgetting to create enough space between an organizer's work

and her life outside that work. For myself, the clearest sign that I needed a break was when I became impatient with everyone. I would show up at work, not listen fully to people's concerns, rush through whatever I was doing, and go home feeling unsatisfied. When I began as an organizer, I would struggle through a few days of this before correctly identifying what was going on, but now I can sense the feelings of burnout emerging much sooner and can extinguish them just as quickly (usually) with a break of a few days, or—if a break is impossible at that moment—by slowing down, breathing deeply, and remembering that I'm in this for the long haul.

In the past (and, to a lesser extent, today), organizing had a certain macho aspect to it, placing demands upon an organizer that forced him to give up any semblance of a personal life for "the cause." I'm thankful that we've finally realized that living solely for the cause can create some pretty unpleasant people, and most organizations now understand that organizers are more effective when they are able to live full lives apart from their professional activities. As well, organizations are recognizing that organizers deserve decent salaries and benefits and that if we want to retain people, they need to be compensated fairly for their work.*

OVERCOMING THE PERFECT STANDARD

Another phenomenon that can cause people to burn out is what Paul Rogat Loeb calls the "perfect standard." "Though we should know better," he writes, "we sometimes feel we have to tackle everything at once. If our efforts don't instantly achieve dramatic results, we are quick to criticize ourselves, and doubt that our efforts can matter."[7]

---

* One particularly absurd example of paying organizers poorly comes from a friend who was working for an organization that was spearheading a living wage campaign. She was putting in long hours, going door-to-door for much of the day to talk to people about the need for the bill. After a few months, however, she had to change jobs, because the organization she was working for paid just above the minimum wage and offered no benefits.

I address this problem of the perfect standard in more depth in Chapter 9, but it does deserve mention here because it can be an easy way to guarantee burnout. The obvious truth is that we're not perfect, and acknowledging imperfection can keep us from becoming frustrated with our work due to unrealistic expectations. As Loeb writes:

> If we don't acknowledge our doubts about particular approaches or causes, the gap between our internal psychological state and our outward allegiances will eventually erode our will to act. The former Vietnam-era activists interviewed by Jack Whalen and Richard Flacks consistently cited ways that the movements they'd joined had discouraged them from expressing fears, misgivings, or feelings of inadequacy. "If one's collective embarked on an organizing project," write Whalen and Flacks, "members expected each other to become instant organizers, free of anxiety about talking to strangers, confidently able to argue a position publicly, perfectly at ease in roles that most people would find intimidating. . . . Activists who had belonged to such collectives are likely to recall the experience as painful because of the unacknowledged gap between public profession and private feeling—and the shame and guilt that resulted." When movements don't allow hesitation, uncertainty, ambivalence, they make it almost impossible for many of their most dedicated participants to continue.[8]

The question of burnout, then, can usually be solved by taking time off, making an effort to create some healthy space between the personal and professional, remembering that organizing is an endurance activity, accepting (even celebrating) our own imperfection, and honestly acknowledging the many doubts we have. Of course, if an organizer attempts to do all of this, and still feels discouraged about her work, then there is always the possibility that it is time to shift jobs or change fields entirely.

THE UNKNOWN PAY-OFFS:
Staying Positive Despite the Evidence

It's important to keep in mind, when door knocking, having meetings, and holding one-on-ones, that positive results of your labor may not surface for some time. In the case of Michael and Millie (discussed in Chapter 2), which garnered such positive media coverage, they first came to PACC because we had done extensive outreach on their block and they knew we helped stop unfair evictions. If we hadn't engaged in so much door knocking in their neighborhood, holding one-on-one meetings with leaders and handing out flyers and attending the local church, who knows what would have happened to Michael and Millie? Their ordeal could have been nothing more than another hell lived out in private, like many of the other tenants whose negative experiences made up the dark side of the neighborhood's "revitalization."

I have a vivid memory of trudging back to the office after a door knocking session on Franklin Avenue, home to Michael and Millie, in early February. I had been going around to see if people had any housing problems and, I hoped, to enlist them in our campaign for increased code enforcement officers for the neighborhood. It had been a brutal morning, with sleet falling and settling on the streets in dirty clumps. The wind whipped across my face, and I remember my glasses fogging up from the bracing cold each time I entered a building. That morning I recall knocking on more than fifty doors and finding not one person who would give me even a minute of their time to explain why I was outside during such unpleasant weather. It was just one of those depressing days that organizers have to take in stride, and I think I was able not to let it affect me too much.

Fast-forward to Michael and Millie: when people watching the evening news saw their sad story, they didn't know that PACC had spent so much time, in the dead of winter, working in the neighborhood to build relationships and agitate around the issue of displacement. Instead people witnessed an unfair eviction that the community had apparently reacted to spontaneously, something that had happened naturally and without much effort. But the campaign and further development of our organizing efforts that it enabled had occurred because organizers had kept up their efforts, even when a more objective assessment might have concluded that no one in the neighborhood cared much about the plights of low-income tenants.

Let's end by returning to the forgotten civil rights movement photograph mentioned earlier: the two organizers on the porch. What expectations did the South offer them back then for the expansion and enforcement of civil rights for blacks? How confident were they that their efforts were going to end in success?

I ask these questions because there is a tendency to inject a deeper meaning into the past than its participants necessarily felt. After all, who wouldn't have been out there organizing in the South if they knew they were part of a revolutionary movement that would achieve such grand accomplishments?

Putting aside the now-familiar power that the civil rights movement was able to muster, what comes into focus is an overwhelmingly bleak view of the South—a view that many organizers must have felt in their bones. At the time, Mississippi's greatest potential seemed to be in producing large numbers of lynchings. The grotesque nature of the lynching of black men makes for nauseating reading, but a knowledge of the lynchings is crucial in understanding the steely resolve and stubborn optimism needed by any organizer operating in the area. Historian Philip Dray recounts the case of two men, Roosevelt Townes and "Bootjack" McDaniels, who were taken by a mob after a white man had been killed in a store in the Mississippi town of Duck Hill in 1936:

> [A]s Townes and McDaniels were exiting the courthouse under police guard, a mob of about one hundred men muscled the guards aside and seized the prisoners . . . who were put aboard an empty school bus. . . . Sobbing and begging for mercy, the prisoners were dragged from the bus and tied between two pine trees, then whipped with a chain and tortured with the flame from a blowtorch. Both men continued to swear their innocence, but McDaniels ultimately broke down, his screams sending children scurrying to their mothers' side. Once he'd confessed to the crime, he was shot to death. Townes had his eyes gouged out with an ice pick and was then slowly roasted with the torch until he, too, agreed to confess. When he finally uttered the words the mob wanted to hear, he was doused with gasoline and set afire.[9]

If 1936 seemed too distant, then there was the more recent case of Emmett Till from which organizers could draw some depressing and frightening lessons. In 1955 the fourteen-year-old Till made a "provocative" gesture to a white woman in the Mississippi Delta. In response, the husband of the dishonored woman and his friend abducted Till, shot him in the face, and dumped him in the river; when his body was recovered, his skull was so damaged that some concluded he had been hit in the face by an ax as well. After the killers had been exonerated by a Mississippi jury, the two men admitted, hoping to finally clear the air, that they had killed Till—but with good reason. The men explained themselves to a reporter:

> Well, what else could we do? He was hopeless. I'm no bully; I never hurt a nigger in my life. I like niggers—

> in their place. . . . But I just decided it was time a few
> people got put on notice. . . . And when a nigger even
> gets close to mentioning sex with a white woman, he's
> tired o' living.[10]

This was the type of society organizers were challenging.

Mississippi was a state with a government hostile to civil rights for African-Americans, a police force firmly in support of the segregationists, and juries that failed to convict in cases of white murders committed against blacks. So when all these things are considered, we're faced with a simple question: What business did these two young men in the photograph have going door-to-door in the heart of Mississippi with a message of hope? Who were they kidding?

What they were doing was something that all good organizers must do: *stay positive despite the indications available at the time*. Organizers must have a belief that "the way things are" can always transform into something that affords a tad more justice. They also have to be ready to convince others of this vague yet strongly held belief. And on days when such hope seems naïve and foolhardy, organizers need to act as if they believe it to be true. Eventually good things will happen.

The truth is, we don't know the effects of our effort. We do know, however, that without the effort—including the cold days spent knocking on the doors of uninterested neighbors, the poorly attended meetings, the flyers that are handed out only to be immediately thrown in the trash—we are guaranteed that nothing positive will emerge. As community organizers work to build relationships, they need to remember that all of the great social movements occurred because foolish folks had pretended they could overcome impossible odds. But impossible odds have a way of giving way to foolish folks—as long as they stay positive despite the indications available at the time.

Chapter 9

WHAT WE STAND TO GAIN:
The Journey of the Organizer

[An] issue of indubitable importance arises: the fact that certain members of the oppressor class join the oppressed in their struggle for liberation, thus moving from one pole of the contradiction to the other. Theirs is a fundamental role, and has been so throughout the history of this struggle. It happens, however, that as they cease to be exploiters or indifferent spectators or simply the heirs of exploitation and move to the side of the exploited, they almost always bring with them the marks of their origin: their prejudices and their deformations, which include a lack of confidence in the people's ability to think, to want, and to know.
—Paulo Freire[1]

I hope this book has shown that, if nothing else, organizing is wonderful work. It is wonderful work for so many reasons: it builds democracy, develops leaders, holds politicians and corporations accountable, results in the passage of progressive legislation, creates a sense of community among sometimes isolated and fearful residents . . . the list is virtually endless.

But this chapter is not about all that. Before I began working as an organizer in Brooklyn, I read quite a bit about organizing, much of which was helpful. But what I never read about—and learned only by actually organizing—is what a personal gift the vocation is to us, the organizers. It is hard to think of a more personally challenging and rewarding job—simply due to the nature of the work itself, irrespective of the tangible policy benefits that may result. Yes, I became an organizer because I wanted to help shake things up, but in the process I learned a great deal about myself and the person I'm still striving to become. The day-to-day practice of being an organizer, I've come to believe, is one of the most psychologically healthy vocations that exist.

This chapter shifts gears a bit, moving from the tactics of organizing to the personal journey of the individual organizer. First, I want to explore some of the issues that may arise when college-educated and privileged individuals begin to organize in low-income communities and/or communities of color. This, it should be evident, is not a simple subject—and I share my roughly formed ideas here not to lay down any definitive "truths," but to explore some of the tensions and pitfalls that can exist and to encourage readers to begin to think for themselves about these subjects. Continuing to organize in Brooklyn, I realized that this book would be incomplete without tackling head-on some of the difficult issues that have more to do with the privileged organizer than the tactics of organizing. To fail to analyze our position and instead pretend that we are just "doing good" is shortsighted and incomplete, leaving many blind spots that need careful analysis and reflection.

What role can privileged people like me play in working with the poor? How can we work in communities that suffer from conditions we've never encountered in our own lives, in communities that are very different from the ones we come from? When we go out and organize, what are some common mistakes that the over-privileged can make in working with the less fortunate? These questions are ambitious and can seem quite overwhelming.

There is also a whole host of more personal and unbelievably tangled questions. What do we ourselves have to gain by engaging in such work? What motivations do we have, both noble and also inevitably more ego-driven, to organize? How do we keep ourselves from inserting our views too deeply into a battle that must be led by the people most affected? What notions may we have to "unlearn" in the process?

COMING FROM A PRIVILEGED BACKGROUND

Many people who choose to become organizers will find themselves working in communities and among people who have had starkly different life experiences.* I, for example, grew up in a solidly upper-middle-class white family in a safe suburb with access to good schools. None of my needs went unmet—I had clothing, I had food, and I had encouraging and supportive parents. I messed around in high school and received terrible grades but was able to take time off and work while living at home, and when I decided to go to college, my parents paid for my education.

The message of this book is unambiguous: the privileged have a role to play in supporting struggles for social justice. I believe in this as firmly as I believe that the people being affected by problems are the ones who ought to lead the way toward solutions. And yet this book encourages an undeniably tension-inducing proposition: recruit people to participate in community organizing, where many will end up working in neighborhoods with people of different class, racial, and educational backgrounds from

---

* There was a time when the old guard considered the ideal organizer someone who was from outside the community (and usually white, male, and college-educated). We should be thankful that that time has passed. Today many organizations (like PACC) have recruited organizers from within their own membership, and the distinction between "leaders" and "organizers" is no longer so clear. I write this with an eye to people like me simply because this is based on my experiences and focuses on the unique issues that have surfaced during my time.

themselves. Much of organizing—especially when working with people very different from oneself—is tense, and rightly so. This healthy tension is what learning is all about: learning about how to overcome differences, identify common desires, interact with people without condescension, and break down barriers of mistrust.

REASONS FOR THE PRIVILEGED TO ORGANIZE

It seems to me that there are two major reasons for the privileged to work as organizers. The first is that we *can* effectively work with others as organizers to help develop leaders and provide assistance in a secondary role that allows indigenous members to blossom. Thus we can make the world better through our organizing.

Second, and perhaps even more important (at least from our subjective, personal perspective), we, the privileged, get to embark on a journey that makes us more compassionate, humane, well-rounded, and wise—values that frequently bypass the well-off when they forget that everyone else isn't doing fine and fail to realize that their unearned success comes at the expense of others' undeserved failure. Therefore, in simple language, we should organize because it makes the world a better place and it makes us (the privileged) better people. It makes us better people because it forces us to engage in five ongoing projects.

THE FIVE ONGOING PROJECTS OF THE ORGANIZER
The Ongoing Project of Listening

When we go to school, we may occasionally hear what others say but we usually aren't taught to listen much, especially when we've become accustomed to having other people defer to us. The further we travel academically, the more we talk; as we gather more information, experience, and expertise, it seems natural to let everyone know what we think. If we move up the corporate food chain, we enjoy the benefits of being at the top of the hierarchy. We determine the problems, we've got the answers, and we've got the credentials to prove that our answers are correct.

Organizing takes us down a profoundly different path.

If there is one skill that an organizer must have, it is the skill of listening. Whether holding one-on-ones with people, attending community meetings, or door knocking, if the bulk of the time is not spent listening, then one is not behaving as an organizer should.

Why is listening so important? Listening implies that we ourselves don't have the perfect answer—which we don't. If we did, well, then we'd be running for political office or something. Instead, we need to recognize that the people we're working with can develop their own answers—when given the support and necessary training—and that these are the answers that matter. If we learn to master the art of listening, then I'm convinced that we can organize in communities very different from the ones we're used to, dealing with issues we might never have had to confront for ourselves.

But maybe not always. If we're listening diligently and we hear that the community resents an outsider being there, then it might mean that we shouldn't be there. But it also might mean that we're just beginning a long journey in learning how to break down barriers, unlearning some of our own negative conditioning (explored further below), and going through all the necessary work before a level of trust is developed between the organizer and the community.

When I began working in Brooklyn in neighborhoods that were almost entirely nonwhite, I felt awkward and out of place—which I was. Many people questioned what I was doing there, suspicious of my motivations. But I stuck around, and as I continued to listen to people and attempted to work with them in a manner that respected their own abilities to solve their problems, some of this distrust dissipated. Eventually, I think we developed a mutual level of understanding, and now I consider many of the people good friends. We've learned together, and one of the things we've learned is that we can work together.

But if we don't focus on the ongoing project of listening, then we're doomed as organizers. We'll end up talking about our answers, pushing people to accept them, making decisions on our own without accepting input from the people being affected. And then we'll be doing something, for sure, but that something clearly won't be organizing.

The Ongoing Project of Exposure

When Michael Harrington wrote *The Other America* in 1962, many were astonished at his tales of the poverty that so many Americans were struggling with. His book was a wake-up call to comfortable people who, because of the class segregation of the time, were able to believe that poverty had largely been eliminated as a mass phenomenon.

Today in the United States, things have only gotten worse in terms of inequality. Yet the barricades that keep people from understanding the experiences of others have also become more strongly fortified. One can grow up in prosperity, graduate from an elite university, retire in a secluded suburb, and die with a clean conscience without ever having to worry about the struggles going on just out of eyesight (or, at times, quite far out of eyesight).

Though I grew up privileged, my parents ensured that I was exposed to a wide variety of people and places, some of whom lived in quite desperate circumstances. When I was in seventh grade I traveled to India with my family. My father was then at Stanford Business School (but, in his defense, directing the non-profit sector of the school), and he led a group of students as they toured factories and cooperatives, while my mother and I tagged along. As we traveled from place to place, I was generally afraid of the many beggars in the street who asked me for money. When we arrived safely at our five-star hotel, I would immediately turn on the television, or swim in the pool, or do any other normal things that an adolescent boy, looking to forget what he'd just seen, would immerse himself in.

At the end of the two-week tour, we decided to spend six days in Calcutta; my mother was a huge admirer of Mother Theresa and her group, the Missionaries of Charity. As part of the experience, I volunteered at the House of the Destitute and Dying. One might expect from the name that it would be a pretty frightening place for a twelve-year-old. But, oddly, I remember the time fondly. I would go from bed to bed handing out medications, talking to the patients who spoke English, and preparing the food. At the end of the day, though I had witnessed a few blankets being pulled over people who had passed away and heard many others moaning in agony, I felt good about the work I had been able to do.

When we got back to the candlelit and collapsing YMCA where we were staying that evening, I longed to return. I had seen people in situations that I hadn't encountered before and I had a desire to work with them, because it felt like the decent thing to do and left me satisfied. They were not people to be avoided, they were people to talk to and, if possible, to help. I had been exposed to people living in desperate situations and been forced to interact with them, and they turned out to be not all that different from me. The lesson has stuck.

When we realize that people have the same fundamental needs—shelter, medical care, food, emotional support—and we choose to work with others whose needs have gone unmet, we begin to break down the barriers that keep the "other America" hidden. Because the truth is that there really is no other America. The fabulously wealthy America and the America living in poverty are intimately related to each other, and once we begin to recognize this fact, we become forced to choose which side we want to cast our lot with. When we organize, we are exposed daily to the realities facing people who are oppressed in one way or another, and this ongoing exposure allows us better to understand both the problems of our country and our own position of privilege within it.

The Ongoing Project of Unlearning

A simple mind experiment: read the following paragraph, then close your eyes and try to conjure a picture of the type of people being described:

> The residents of the area we are imagining don't work, spending most of their free time either drinking, getting high, or lounging about. Many of the individuals make terrible choices, but there always seems to be someone waiting to come in at the last moment and bail them out. These people seem to think that the world owes them something, that one should do only things that are pleasurable, without realizing that nothing comes in this life without hard work. They wake late every morning, getting up around noon nursing another hangover, and stumble over to a food pantry to get a free meal.

What images do these descriptions conjure? Take a moment and try to create a mental picture of the community being described. What does it look like? Who are these people? Where would we find them?

If you inherited the same cultural baggage as I did, then the image you have in your head probably looks like a typical inner city, whose residents are mostly African-American and Latino. And yet what I was describing, in all seriousness though with a few superficial alterations (I used the term "food pantry" in place of "cafeteria"), was the environment of the small liberal arts university I attended, whose students were mostly white and financially secure.

It's a strange description, for sure, but the strangeness illustrates how much we've got to unlearn. In our society there is so much vilification of the poor (Ronald Reagan set the bar when he coined the term "welfare queen") that even people who try to resist the propaganda have a hard time preventing it from seeping through. So we're accustomed to fearing young black males and may believe that people living in poverty landed there solely due to poor choices and character flaws, but we're not at all likely to generalize about a university as a place where lazy people live off the largesse of the "system."

Even though I grew up in a family that taught me some pretty countercultural ideas (during grade school, for example, my father helped me come up with an alternative to the Army slogan: Be All That You Can Be, Support Poor Families), I've learned through organizing that I still absorbed certain prejudicial ideas. The main one, which probably affects most people who had the luck to grow up privileged, is that the system works. For many who grew up in privilege, the greatest sources of frustration came from relatively minor problems, perhaps on par with the inefficiency of the local DMV. Our struggles were waged against peripheral institutions, institutions providing services that were not critical to our survival. Though they were unpleasant experiences, when all is said and done these institutions get the job done—and if they do mess up completely, no one dies.

This lesson—that the system works—is one of the hardest to unlearn. Integral to this sentiment, often only held unconsciously, is that those who are not on the winning end somehow failed—refused to make the system work for them. Though I try hard to overcome this feeling, I never do completely. But as I continued to work as an organizer in Brooklyn, I regularly witnessed the daily hurdles thrown up in people's paths that I had never needed to worry about. By working directly with people, we go from abstract generalizations about the "underclass" to the realization that behind this generalization are regular families whose needs are going unmet. That's the project of unlearning.

It should be mentioned that the projects of exposure and unlearning are intimately related. When we are exposed to people struggling for things we took for granted, we begin the process of unlearning. These projects help cut through a lot of the sanctimonious bullshit on the lips of politicians when they speak of things like "family values" or "moral choices." In fact, the reasons most of the people I worked with were living in poverty and distress were quite simple and had nothing to do with "values." They worked for people who paid less than was needed to survive, they suffered health problems that a lack of insurance exacerbated, they ended up homeless because the landlord evicted them before they had found a new place that they could afford.

Empty rhetoric about values only obscures the real phenomenon, which is that the system fails people who can't pay enough to make it work for them. It also becomes quite clear that the consequences of laziness are nonexistent for some but unduly harsh for others. To pretend that there is some sort of universal justice that applies equally to all regardless of economic background, race, gender, or sexual preference is just plain ignorant. But it's what we've been taught and so it's what we've got to unlearn.

The Ongoing Project of Humility

Organizers, admittedly, may sometimes appear quite brash; I would hesitate to characterize many personalities I have come across (including mine) as unwaveringly humble. There are moments when organizers may provoke strong reactions, prod their members, and make grandiose claims. But, still, a profound core value of organizing is humility. This humility comes out of a belief that ordinary people affected by issues have the power and ability to come up with their own answers, and that holds the estimation of one's importance at the same level as that of others. To live up to this organizing creed requires constant vigilance on the organizers' part, so that we do not begin speaking "for" people or "telling" them the solutions as if they have no right to debate and determine their fates for themselves. It also acknowledges that we are constantly learning, refining, adapting—in short, being surprised—and that we are on a path with uncertain ends and no agreed-upon solution.

Because organizing depends upon a belief that the people being affected by issues are the ones most qualified to lead, we have an ongoing project of learning to be humble. This doesn't mean that we must be meek, or acquiescent, or bottle up our emotions to make sure we don't influence others—all of these things are unhealthy and ultimately unsustainable. Instead I'm speaking of the humane and rare value of believing that we have much more to learn than to teach. In a world that tells us that the privileged—because of our education level, ethnic background, sexual orientation, gender, or income—are extraordinary and have much to contribute to the world, organizing forces us to remember that others do, too.

The Ongoing Project of Living with Imperfection

While I was finishing up this book, I met a woman on a plane. I had left the manuscript on my seat, and on my return she asked me if I was writing a dissertation or some similarly tortuous document. I explained to her that I was attempting to write a book, and when she seemed interested, I asked if she'd be open to reading some of it and giving me feedback.

She read the introduction and first chapter and told me that she liked it but that she herself had never gotten into organizing or progressive work of any kind, though she was sympathetic to the cause.

"The school I went to was very liberal," she told me. "We had students working to support the workers in the cafeteria, which I agreed with, but I couldn't enjoy being around the 'holier than thou' crowd. I wasn't vegetarian, which was a big problem, too, 'cause many of the people were hard-core animal-rights activists. So I never really got involved."

She was working in the music industry, something she really enjoyed, and it was apparent that music was her first calling. Still, her experiences of feeling shut out are far from uncommon. Many college students interested in getting into activism have had the experience of being made to feel uncomfortable because their views were not progressive or radical enough. In my experience, people who most fervently toe this demanding line live in a very neat universe, interacting with others of similar backgrounds who hold nearly identical views. When someone enters this circle without the accepted opinions, she is made to feel like a failure. These "radicals" have the answers all sorted out and interpret any wavering or disagreement as a sign of a fatal character flaw.

There are a lot of things that this type of morally pure thinking is not. Among other things, it is not generous, not compassionate, not human, and not healthy. It is disconnected from people as they are actually found in the world—with infinite variety, quite complicated, frequently confused—and attempts to boil everything down to a tidy and deadening political platform. This unhealthy sense of moral perfection, however, is challenged when one goes out into the real world and begins organizing.

An early lesson to learn is that we as organizers are far, far, far from perfect—and acknowledging this imperfection outright makes it a lot less likely that we'll become an annoying or conceited martyr, who carries a huge cross on our back that we feel the need to share whenever possible. My motivations for organizing revolve around my desire to help create a better world, but I also take pride in my accomplishments and hope to get recognition for my work. When we hold a direct action, I am genuinely moved when our members get to express themselves, but I also get an egotistical thrill from seeing myself quoted in the media. When we get involved with organizing, we learn that human motivations are frequently far from perfect, but we learn to live with this imperfection.

Through the project of living with imperfection we learn that we don't have to wait until we've sorted out all our internal conflicts or somehow become morally "pure" before we can make a positive difference. Indeed, had I felt the need to wait until I was absolutely convinced of my ability to organize and to do so without any feelings of contradiction or conflict, then I'd still be sitting around watching television and mentally beating myself up every night. Instead, through taking action I've come a long way in terms of achieving concrete positive results with our community members, learning how to be more compassionate, and coming to terms with my own imperfections. There is no morally pure universe out there, no special way to plug into a simple existence of total satisfaction and conviction. But when we organize, we learn to live with imperfection by . . . well, living with imperfection.

And it should be said that even with all this imperfection, wonderful things still occur. Imperfect people acting at times on imperfect motives can nevertheless accomplish remarkable feats. The image we hold of activists and organizers is often one of blemish-free puritans born with a superhuman ability to do the right thing at all times, seeming to live in a foreign world free from contradiction or worry. But as Paul Rogat Loeb writes in *Soul of a Citizen,* in the nicely titled chapter "We Don't Have to be Saints":

> *When we do act, others may view us as heroic knights riding in to save the day, but we're more like knights on rickety tricycles, clutching our fears and hesitations as we go. . . . How then, shall we characterize those who participate in our society as active citizens? They are people*

of imperfect character, acting on the basis of imperfect
knowledge, for causes that may be imperfect as well. I
could be mistaken, but I think that's a profile any of us
could match, given a willingness to live with ambiguity
and all it implies, including occasional failure and frus-
tration. That kind of imperfection may not be saintly, but
living with it in the service of justice is a virtue.[2]

This imperfection, it should be added, is applied liberally across the population; by no means is it confined to just the organizer. As soon as one starts organizing in poor communities, one realizes that the poor are not some sort of romanticized class that can do no wrong. They are, in fact, just as human as the fabulously wealthy and the ridiculously privileged. They are individuals who have had more obstacles thrown in their paths and so have learned more about what problems need to be fixed, but they also hold their own sorts of prejudices, as every other group does. They are not inanimate objects: neither the caricatured images of perfection espoused by some revolutionaries nor the degraded and worthless people portrayed by right-wing ideologues. They are, obviously, human.

So, to summarize, we've got absolutely flawed people across the board. I'm a frequently selfish organizer, working with frequently selfish community members. To pretend otherwise is to miss a big piece of the reality in which we find ourselves. But there's also this core belief, vague and difficult to be precise about—but paradoxically more concrete than any other—that calls us to work with others who are similarly moved in the fight for social justice. We're flawed and yet we're beautiful and capable of incredible things; it's a more difficult reality to come to grips with than the neat and unambiguous images of revolution and crisp moral perfection—but it's also, to me, somehow more hopeful.

The Ongoing Project of Developing Empathy

Organizing is a great way to begin to learn about the world as it exists, through direct experience. These direct experiences teach us lessons very different from the simple obligation to help others. Organizing does not teach us in some abstract manner that the poor have harder lives than the wealthy—any left-leaning teenager can understand as much. It does not immerse us in the type of guilt that comes from knowing that starving people in Africa could benefit from the leftovers we toss into the trash. It does not simply strengthen our sense of sympathy, the kind of sympathy that comes when one steps over a sleeping person in the street and wishes one could help. In our frequently alienated lives, a distant sense of sympathy for others in trouble is not rare. We all know that homeless people should have homes, that the hungry should be able to eat, that the sick should be able to access quality health care.

But this sense of guilt, sympathy, and pain keeps the unfortunate separated from us, as people we should "help" out of a sense of obligation, usually by contributing in impersonal ways like writing checks or donating food. It feels good, sure, and it does truly help. But it doesn't cultivate the sense of empathy that one develops by actually working *with* others, by getting to know the underprivileged as people and, sometimes, good friends. Organizing forces the organizer outside of her comfort zone, into direct contact with types of people she might never encounter or develop meaningful relationships with otherwise. It develops not only sympathy but empathy, an empathy that finally realizes—spiritually, not intellectually—that the poor are not at arm's length with problems unrelated to our lives. We are privileged because they are oppressed. The same market that has granted us homes has kept others homeless. We receive quality education and others must sit in overcrowded classrooms with out-of-date textbooks. In sum, our society has rewarded us richly for work we didn't do and punished others without reason or rationale. It is not from a sense of guilt that we need to reform the system, but from a sense of justice. The system has allowed some to go to college, to live comfortably, to enjoy a type of freedom alien to many, and this means that we have a duty to help undo the system until everyone has the same opportunity. While we do so, our sense of empathy—the ability to understand and share the feelings of another—will grow. This empathy, perhaps *the* defining characteristic of healthy human beings, is the greatest gift we as organizers can receive.

———————

I will end by recounting a story from the civil rights movement. All movements for social justice contain countless stories of everyday heroism, sacrifice, compassion, and solidarity, and I like to return to such stories to remember the potential for transformation that can lie just below the surface of apparently insurmountable injustices.

It was the first day of the Montgomery Bus Boycott. An exhausted woman walking along the street is offered a ride by a minister, who asks if she is tired. She replies, "Well, my body may be tired, but for many years my soul has been tired. Now my soul is resting. So I don't mind if my body is tired, because my soul is free."[3]

Organizing, I can attest, is tiring. Long hours of work are put in, day after day. Often this work may seem pointless. Often no gains are made. Often things fall apart.

But sometimes they don't. When they don't, one has a peek into a more democratic world, one where people are able to live with dignity, are able to satisfy their basic human needs, and are afforded the ability to hope for something better. To witness this process, to help bring it along, is why I organize. To make it one's life is grand.

Organizing 101: A Glossary of Terms

Accountability Session:

A meeting (large, it is hoped) to which a group invites the target (most often a politician) to clearly spell out a demand. The point is for the target to either say "yes" or "no" right then and there and to demonstrate to the target that many people are concerned about the issue and are there to witness his or her reaction (and vote accordingly).

Base:

Most simply, the members of an organization. An organization with a base is one that can mobilize its members to take direct action. Social service and advocacy groups do not usually have a base—it is generally a unique characteristic of organizing groups.

Base-building:

The process of recruiting new members to the organization, usually through door knocking. Many organizations use certain months of the year to do their base-building (for example, summer), so that when they ratchet up their campaign, they will have the members needed to make an impact.

Congregation-based organizing:

Also known as church-based organizing. Congregation-based organizing uses religious institutions, developing leaders within congregations that can work on areas of concern, sometimes in partnership with other religious groups. There are many advantages to working within congregations; most obviously, an organizer will already have a base of members to work with, and the task is less base-building than leadership development.

Fund-raising:

Most organizations receive the bulk of their money from foundations and the government. Foundations often advertise Requests for Proposals (RFPs), which highlight the types of work they're looking to fund in the coming year. Sometimes their criteria are broad (building leadership within low-income communities) and at other times specific (organizing youth around education issues). Often a community-based organization will have a grant writer who is responsible for crafting proposals, working in concert with the organizers. If there is a director of organizing, it can also be that director's task to do the bulk of the writing, since he or she knows the issues the best.

Many organizations also receive funding from various government sources (city, state, federal). Care should be taken when responding to RFPs from the government, however, as accepting government funds can compromise the organizing work. For example, a housing group that receives funding from city government (as PACC does) may tone down its demands and organizing activities that target the city. In addition, reporting requirements for the government may be so laborious and the work so independent of the group's mission that although funds may be coming in, they do nothing to further the group's goals. There is no reason to receive money if that money isn't going to be paying for anything worthwhile.

Grassroots fund-raising:

The practice of bringing in money not through foundations or government agencies but by raising funds from the community. This can be done through local events such as benefit concerts, fashion shows, fund-raising dinners, and phone-banking drives to solicit funds and membership. This type of fund-raising is critical as it brings in money that can be used for whatever purpose the organization deems fit, without strings attached, and can be a steady source of income during an economic downturn when foundations and the government become tightfisted. ACORN is an example of a very effective organization in terms of grassroots fund-raising, raising the bulk of its money from membership dues.

Handle:

A "handle" is essentially a way to frame an issue and talk about it publicly, providing a quick context that makes the need for change clear. When Make the Road by Walking sought to challenge New York City's lack of translation services, talking about the issue as a violation of people's civil rights created a handle both to recruit new members to the work and to solicit interest from politicians and the media.

Institution-based organizing:

Like congregation-based organizing, but including secular groups. Institution-based organizing, a model championed by Saul Alinsky, seeks to combine already existing groups into a coalition that can act as one. The advantages of this approach are easy to discern: when an organizer already has various bases to work with, the task is to focus on the leaders of each base to hash out a common agenda.

Membership:

A more complicated term than one might think; in a membership-based or -driven organization, people who join—usually by paying dues—are collectively the engine that decides the actions of the organization. The formal by-laws of a membership organization will, among other things, mandate that members vote to elect the board of directors, who then govern the group's priorities. Although the dues raised by membership help with grassroots fund-raising, the most important aspect is not the money raised but the communication of an idea: the members *own* the organization and can hold their leaders accountable.

Participatory action research:

Research conducted by members and organizers that compiles information needed to inform or move a campaign. The organization uses its own people to do the research and builds into this work such practices as membership recruitment. Especially helpful in documenting problems that agencies have overlooked and in legitimizing campaign demands.

Reports:

Not a new term, but it bears mentioning because reports can be an easy way to achieve media coverage. If you're working on health issues, for example, and you find that a number of members with whom you're working suffer from asthma, you can create a report profiling some of the members, identifying likely culprits (poor housing conditions, perhaps, or a nearby bus depot where vehicles idle for hours), and positing a solution. And the more reports you write, the easier they become.

Turf:

For neighborhood-based organizing, a turf is the geographic area that an organizer focuses on. Randomly knocking on doors will quickly come to feel inconsequential and overwhelming, so splitting an area into turfs makes the task more manageable. During one summer door-knocking effort, for example, we had six organizers on the doors five days a week, each with his or her own set of blocks on which to focus. Record-keeping is key.

Turnout:

An easy enough term to understand: the number of people who show up for a given event. For individual organizations with multiple organizers, each person can be assigned a turnout goal for an upcoming meeting or action, which is the number of their contacts they will be responsible for activating. When working with coalitions of other organizations, each group will often have to commit to how many members it will turn out for actions. Some actions—such as accountability sessions—demand a large turnout. Others can be more targeted and might only need a dozen people (it's unbelievable how much ruckus twelve people can make in certain environments).

Resources and Opportunities for Future Organizers

Below are brief descriptions and links to organizations that provide information, training, internships, and employment opportunities for future organizers. The organizations range from union- and neighborhood-based to congregation-based, and many have online applications. Good luck!

AFL-CIO: Union Summer

The labor movement is always looking for organizers. Since 1996, the AFL-CIO has been running a Union Summer program based upon SNCC's Freedom Summer campaign; the program is a ten-week internship for people interested in working in the labor movement (I completed a Union Summer internship in Denver, and it was great fun). Participants receive a stipend and free lodging and are placed with unions around the country.

For more information about participating in Union Summer, call 1-888-835-8557 or e-mail: unionsummer@aflcio.org. You can also read more about the program at http://www.aflcio.org.

AFL-CIO: Organizing Institute (OI)

For individuals already convinced they want to become labor organizers, the Organizing Institute provides an intensive three-day training, after which the graduate meets with OI staff to discuss future job possibilities. Future training sessions and locations are available online, as is an application.

For more information and to apply to the OI, go to http://www.aflcio.org /aboutus/oi/3daytraining.cfm.

Association of Community Organizations for Reform Now (ACORN)

ACORN is the nation's largest community organization of low- and moderate-income families, with more than 220,000 member families throughout seventy-five U.S. cities. They are well-known for their confrontation tactics and organize around a vast number of issues, including predatory lending, living wages, health care, and better schools. An online application is available at the ACORN Web site, as is a phone number.

For more information, go to http://www.acorn.org.

Center for Third World Organizing (CTWO)

The Center for Third World Organizing, a racial justice organization dedicated to building a social justice movement led by people of color, is a twenty-year-old training and resource center that promotes and sustains direct-action organizing in communities of color in the United States. CTWO is best known for its Movement Activist Apprenticeship Program (MAAP), which connects people of color with organizing internships with groups across the country. An online application for MAAP is available at the CTWO Web site.

For more information, go to http://www.ctwo.org.

Direct Action and Research Training Center (DART)

DART engages in congregation-based organizing and currently has affiliates in Florida, Indiana, Kentucky, Michigan, Ohio, and Virginia. It runs an organizing institute for future organizers, which includes a weeklong training course and is followed by four months of organizing alongside a mentor in one of the affiliate organizations (both the training and mentored organizing are paid).

For more information and to apply online, go to http://www.thedart center.org.

Idealist.org

Idealist.org is a vast clearinghouse of job openings, internships, and volunteer opportunities, with information about more than sixty thousand listed nonprofit and community organizations around the world. To search for current openings in organizing groups, under the term Job Category enter "Activism & Organizing." You can also search by Area of Focus, which allows you to find, for example, organizing jobs dealing with issues of immigration (it's where I found my job in Brooklyn).

For more information, go to http://www.idealist.org.

Industrial Areas Foundation (IAF)

The IAF, founded by Saul Alinsky and then matured under Edward Chambers, has affiliates in twenty-one states and engages in institution-based organizing (primarily with congregations). The IAF focuses on issues such as a living wage and affordable housing. It offers summer internships and ninety-day paid tryouts for interested individuals, who—if successful—will be offered full-time organizing positions.

For more information, go to http://www.industrialareasfoundation.org.

Midwest Academy

One of the nation's oldest and best-known schools for community organizations, citizen organizations, and individuals committed to progressive social change. The Midwest Academy offers five-day training sessions for leaders and staff of community organizations, and its Web site also has a job bank for organizing positions. The academy is the publisher of *Organize!* one of the best books on organizing techniques.

For more information, go to http://www.midwestacademy.com.

National Organizers Alliance

An organization that seeks to connect and share skills between organizers, NOA's mission is to advance progressive organizing for social, economic, and environmental justice and to sustain, support, and nurture the people of all ages who do it. NOA also has a job bank for organizing positions.

For more information, go to http://www.noacentral.org.

The Online Conference on Community Organizing and Development (COMM-ORG)

COMM-ORG is a Web site with tons of information related to community organizing, including opinion papers from both academics and community organizers. It also has links to national and local groups involved in organizing as well as places that provide training and technical assistance.

For more information, go to http://comm-org.wisc.edu.

PICO

PICO is a national network of faith-based community organizations working to create innovative solutions to problems facing urban, suburban, and rural communities. Since 1972, PICO has successfully worked to increase access to health care, improve public schools, make neighborhoods safer, build affordable housing, redevelop communities, and revitalize democracy. A list of current job openings and a contact for employment opportunities are available on the PICO Web site.

For more information, go to http://www.piconetwork.org.

Wellstone Action

Wellstone Action is a national center for training and leadership development for the progressive movement. Wellstone Action's mission is to honor the legacy of Paul and Sheila Wellstone by continuing their work through training, educating, mobilizing, and organizing a vast network of progressive individuals and organizations. Wellstone Action runs several training programs, focused on combining grassroots organizing, electoral organizing, progressive public policy, and ethical leadership. Along with its weekend-long Camp Wellstone, it also runs Campus Wellstone, for college activists, and a Voter Engagement School, which works with community-based organizations to integrate electoral work into their local organizing campaigns.

For more information, go to http://www.wellstone.org.

Further Reading

On Organizing

Alinsky, Saul. *Reveille for Radicals* (New York: Vintage Books, 1989).

————. *Rules for Radicals: A Pragmatic Primer for Realistic Radicals* (New York: Vintage Books, 1989).

> Two classic studies in the motivations and methods of organizers. Though Alinsky certainly had his blind spots, these books are still mandatory reading material for folks starting out.

Bobo, Kim, Jerry Kendall, and Steve Max. *Organize! Organizing for Social Change* (Santa Ana: Seven Locks Press, 2001).

> Probably the most complete "how-to" guide on community organizing, authored by organizers from the Midwest Academy. Includes helpful guidance on nuts-and-bolts items such as facilitating meetings, speaking in public, and working within coalitions.

Delgado, Gary. *Beyond the Politics of Place: New Directions in Community Organizing* (Berkeley: Chardon Press, 1997).

> Delgado, the former director of the Center for Third World Organizing, looks at the evolving practices of community organizing, with a special focus on groups headed by people of color and the alternative models to Alinsky that they have adopted.

Fisher, Robert. *Let the People Decide: Neighborhood Organizing in America* (New York: Twayne Publishers, 1994).

> Fisher gives the reader a comprehensive historical overview of neighborhood-based community organizing in the United States, with useful insights on the various models of organizing.

Freire, Paulo. *Pedagogy of the Oppressed* (New York: Continuum, 1994).

> A classic. Freire clearly outlines the libratory potential of participatory education relevant to community organizers.

Gecan, Michael. *Going Public: An Inside Story of Disrupting Politics as Usual* (Boston: Beacon Press, 2002).

> A memoir written by an Industrial Areas Foundation organizer who has spent years working with East Brooklyn Congregations provides a clear introduction to the philosophy of IAF organizing.

Gordon, Jennifer. *Suburban Sweatshops: The Fight for Immigrant Rights* (Cambridge, MA: Harvard University Press, 2005).

> Gordon founded the Long Island–based Workplace Project in 1992 and was its director for six years (she is now a professor of law at Fordham University). Her book recounts her years spent organizing Latino immigrant day laborers and also serves as a valuable meditation on the challenges and promise of combining organizing with advocacy.

Horwitz, Sanford D. *Let Them Call Me Rebel: Saul Alinsky, His Life and Legacy* (New York: Vintage, 1992).

> A well-researched biography of Saul Alinsky that sheds light on the development of his ideas on organizing.

Sen, Rinku. *Stir It Up: Lessons in Community Organizing and Advocacy* (San Francisco: Jossey-Bass, 2003).

> Sen, who spent many years with the Center for Third World Organizing, provides an overview of modern-day organizing techniques and philosophies. Included throughout the book are case studies of a wide variety of organizations to highlight key points.

Shaw, Randy. *The Activist's Handbook: A Primer* (Berkeley: University of California Press, 2001).

> An informative and engaging text. Especially illuminating are the many case studies that Shaw includes, exploring previous campaigns concerned with issues such as homelessness, HIV/AIDS, and environmental justice.

Stout, Linda. *Bridging the Class Divide and Other Lessons for Grassroots Organizing* (Boston: Beacon Press, 1996).

> Part memoir and part model for future organizing, Linda Stout's book is an inspiring and accessible read that focuses on the need for more organizers to come from within the communities affected and calls for awareness of the many ways low-income people are made to feel uncomfortable (intentionally or not) by upper-income organizers.

Wellstone, Paul. *How the Rural Poor Got Power: Narrative of a Grass-Roots Organizer* (Minneapolis: University of Minnesota Press, 2003).

> I found this book only recently and was immediately impressed by Wellstone's clear writing style and unflinching honesty. The book centers around Wellstone's work with the Organization for a Better Rice County, located in rural Minnesota, and includes enlightening interviews with participants.

On Fund-raising

Klein, Kim. *Fundraising for Social Change.* (San Francisco: Jossey-Bass, 2007).

> The definitive book on how to raise money for progressive organizations.

On Media

Bray, Roberts. *Spin Works! A Media Guidebook for Communicating Values and Shaping Opinion* (San Francisco: Independent Media Institute, 2002).

> A thin volume loaded with helpful information on everything from writing press releases to successfully developing relationships with reporters. They also run a Web site, http://www.spinproject.org.

Salzman, Jason. *Making the News: A Guide for Activists and Nonprofits* (Boulder: Westview Press, 2003).

> A comprehensive guide that together with *Spin Works!* will teach just about every lesson organizers need as they work to publicize their activities.

On History, Social Movements, and Democracy

Brecher, Jeremy. *Strike!* (Cambridge, MA: South End Press, 1997).

> Originally published in 1972, this updated classic chronicles the tumultuous labor history of the United States, told from the perspective of rank-and-file workers.

Dubofsky, Melvyn. *We Shall Be All: A History of the Industrial Workers of the World* (Urbana and Chicago: University of Illinois Press, 2000).

> The IWW was a militant and antiracist labor organization founded in 1905 dedicated not only to winning higher wages but the elimination of bosses altogether. Popularly known as "Wobblies," they were determined to organize *all* working people–including African Americans, immigrants, and migrant workers–into "one big union," and won numerous direct action campaigns. It is helpful to remember that the country of George W. Bush also gave birth to such a radical, egalitarian movement.

Goodwyn, Lawrence. *The Populist Moment: A Short History of the Agrarian Revolt in America* (New York: Oxford University Press, 1978).
> Goodwyn's book covers an inspiring and largely unknown period in U.S. history and includes a profound discussion on the nature of building democratic movements.

Honey, Michael K. *Going Down Jericho Road: The Memphis Strike, Martin Luther King's Last Campaign* (New York: W.W. Norton & Company, 2007).
> Fabulous history of the 1968 sanitation worker strike in Memphis, organized by African-American rank-and-file members. King was assassinated in Memphis while supporting the strike, which he hoped would spark a broad "Poor People's Campaign" for economic equality. Honey does an exemplary job examining the symbiotic relationship between civil rights leaders like King and mass movements, while chronicling the difficulties in shifting the movement's focus from civil rights to economic justice.

Lummis, C. Douglas. *Radical Democracy* (Ithaca, NY: Cornell University Press, 1996)
> I've yet to find a better book about the promise of democracy.

Marable, Manning. *Black Leadership* (New York: Columbia University Press, 1998).
> Marable's discussion on black leadership offers many keen insights into leadership as a whole and what type of leadership is appropriate for democratic mass movements.

McAdam, Doug. *Freedom Summer* (New York: Oxford University Press, 1988).
> McAdam traces the effects that the 1964 Freedom Summer campaign in Mississippi had on its participants. Demonstrates the power that an early organizing experience can have in determining an individual's life trajectory, and corrects the conventional wisdom that 1960s radicals all later became disillusioned sell-outs.

Payne, Charles M. *I've Got the Light of Freedom: The Organizing Tradition and the Mississippi Freedom Struggle* (Berkeley: University of California Press, 1995).

> With so many books about the civil rights movement focusing on well-known leaders, Payne reminds us that the real key to its victories lay in the determined actions of mostly-forgotten citizens.

Piven, Frances Fox, and Richard A. Cloward. *Poor People's Movements: Why They Succeed, How They Fail.* (New York: Vintage Books, 1979)

> A very challenging book that questions prevailing orthodoxy about the types of organizations and organizing models that lead to social change.

Ransby, Barbara. *Ella Baker and the Black Freedom Movement: A Radical Democratic Vision* (Chapel Hill: University of North Carolina Press, 2003).

> A superb biography on one of the greatest organizers in American history.

Robinson, Jo Ann Gibson. *The Montgomery Bus Boycott and the Women Who Started It: The Memoir of Jo Ann Gibson Robinson* (Knoxville: University of Tennessee Press, 1987).

> A short memoir that reclaims one of the greatest direct-action campaigns for the people who actually organized it: African-American women.

Zinn, Howard. *A People's History of the United States: 1492–Present* (New York: HarperCollins, 1995).

———. *The Politics of History* (Urbana and Chicago: University of Illinois Press, 1990).

———. *SNCC: The New Abolitionists* (Boston: Beacon Press, 1967).

> Zinn's books are fantastic reminders that the most important history is made by the often-forgotten underdogs.

Notes

Introduction

1. Simeon Strunsky, *No Mean City* (New York: Dutton, 1944), cited in C. Douglas Lummis, *Radical Democracy* (Ithaca: Cornell University Press, 1996), p. 8.
2. Cited in Chuck Collins and Felice Yeskel, *Economic Apartheid in America* (New York: New Press, 2000), p. 54.
3. Holly Sklar, Laryssa Mykyta, and Susan Wefald, *Raise the Floor: Wages and Policies That Work for All of Us* (Cambridge, MA: South End Press, 2001), p. 59.
4. Barbara Kingsolver, *Animal Dreams* (New York: Harper & Row, 1980), p. 299.
5. Lummis, *Radical Democracy,* p. 15.

Chapter 1

1. Si Kahn, *Organizing: A Guide for Grassroots Leaders* (New York: McGraw-Hill, 1982), p. 1.

2. Michael Gecan, *Going Public: An Inside Story of Disrupting Politics as Usual* (Boston: Beacon Press, 2002), p. 9.
3. Saul Alinsky, *Rules for Radicals: A Pragmatic Primer for Realistic Radicals* (New York: Vintage Books, 1972), p. 21.
4. Peter R. Mitchell and John Schoeffel, *Understanding Power: The Indispensable Chomsky* (New York: New Press, 2002), p. 186.
5. Linda Stout, *Bridging the Class Divide: And Other Lessons of Grassroots Organizing* (Boston: Beacon Press, 1996), p. 106.
6. Rinku Sen, *Stir It Up: Lessons in Community Organizing and Advocacy* (San Francisco: Jossey-Bass, 2003), p. 43.
7. Jennifer Gordon, *Suburban Sweatshops: The Fight for Immigrant Rights* (Cambridge, MA: Harvard University Press, 2005), pp. 193–94.

Chapter 2

1. William Dunhoff, *The Power Elite and the State: How Policy Is Made in America* (New York: Aldine de Gruyter, 1990), cited in Anders Corr, *No Trespassing! Squatting, Rent Strikes, and Land Struggles Worldwide* (Cambridge, MA): South End Press, 1999), p. 77.
2. Quoted in Kim Bobo, Jackie Kendall, and Steve Max, *Organize! Organizing for Social Change* (Santa Ana: Seven Locks Press, 2001). The full text of Douglass's statement is worth quoting:

> *Let me give you a word on the philosophy of reform. The whole history of the progress of human liberty shows that all concessions yet made to her august claims have been born of earnest struggle. The conflict has been exciting, agitating, all absorbing, and for the time being putting all other tumults to silence. It must do this or it does nothing. If there is no struggle there is no progress. Those who profess to favor freedom, and depreciate agitation, are men who want crops without plowing up the ground. They want rain without thunder and lightning.*

They want the ocean without the awful roar of its many waters. This struggle may be a moral one; or it may be a physical one; or it may be both moral and physical; but it must be a struggle. Power concedes nothing without a demand. It never did and it never will. Find out just what people will submit to, and you have found the exact amount of injustice and wrong which will be imposed upon them; and these will continue until they are resisted with either words or blows, or with both. The limits of tyrants are prescribed by the endurance of those whom they oppress.

3. Howard Zinn, *A People's History of the United States, 1492–Present* (New York: HarperCollins, 1995), p. 634.
4. Sen, *Stir It Up,* p. 96.
5. Randy Shaw, *The Activist's Handbook* (Berkeley: University of California Press, 2001), p. 212.
6. Alinsky, *Rules for Radicals,* pp. 127, 130.
7. Shaw, *Activist's Handbook,* p. 212.
8. David Garrow, *Bearing the Cross* (New York: William Morrow, 1986), p. 625.

Chapter 3

1. Gecan, *Going Public,* pp. 21–22.
2. Quoted in Lee Staples, *Roots to Power: A Manual for Grassroots Organizing* (Westport, CT: Praeger, 1984), p. 120.
3. Jim Hightower, "The Wellstone Way," *The Nation,* January 27, 2003.
4. Charles M. Payne, *I've Got the Light of Freedom: The Organizing Tradition and the Mississippi Freedom Struggle* (Berkeley: University of California Press, 1995), p. 3.

Chapter 4

1. Full text of speech is available online at the Eugene V. Debs Internet Archive: http://www.marxists.org/archive/debs/works/1918/canton.htm.

2. Sen, *Stir It Up,* p. 97.

3. Quoted in Barbara Ransby, *Ella Baker and the Black Freedom Movement: A Radical Democratic Vision* (Chapel Hill: University of North Carolina Press, 2003), p. 188.

4. Ransby, *Ella Baker and the Black Freedom Movement,* p. 193.

5. Linda Stout, *Bridging the Class Divide,* p. 142.

6. Gerder Lerner, "Developing Community Leadership," in *Black Women in White America* (New York: Pantheon, 1972), p. 347.

7. Ibid., p. 347.

8. Ransby, *Ella Baker and the Black Freedom Movement,* p. 270.

9. Carol Mueller, "Ella Baker and the Origins of 'Participatory Democracy,'" in *Women in the Civil Rights Movement: Trailblazers and Torchbearers, 1941–1965* (New York: Carlson Publishing, 1990), p. 64.

10. Full text of speech is available online at the Eugene V. Debs Internet Archive: http://www.marxists.org/archive/debs/works/1905/industrial.htm.

11. Stout, *Bridging the Class Divide,* p. 155.

12. Doug McAdam, *Freedom Summer* (New York: Oxford University Press, 1988), p. 164.

13. Kenneth J. Heineman, *Put Your Bodies upon the Wheels: Student Revolt in the 1960s* (Chicago: Ivan R. Dee, 2001), quoted on opening page (no number).

14. Robert Fisher, *Let the People Decide* (New York: Twayne Publications, 1997), pp. 227–28.

15. Paulo Freire, *Pedagogy of the Oppressed* (New York: Continuum, 1994), pp. 53–54.

16. Ibid., pp. 64, 62.

17. Alinsky, *Rules for Radicals,* p. 79.

18. A good overview of Alinsky's experiences in Chicago can be found in Sanford Horwitz, *Let Them Call Me Rebel: Saul Alinsky, His Life and Legacy* (New York: Knopf, 1989).

19. Sen, *Stir It Up,* p. lxiii.

20. Carol Bly, *Changing the Bully Who Rules the World: Reading and Thinking About Ethics* (Minneapolis: Milkweed Editions, 1996), p. 34.

Chapter 5

1. Bobo, Kendall, and Max, *Organize!* p. 165.

2. Ibid., p. 163.

3. Sen, *Stir It Up,* p. 126.

4. Ibid., p. 118.

Chapter 7

1. John Keane, *Democracy and Civil Society* (London: Verso, 1998), cited in James Green, *Taking History to Heart: The Power of the Past in Building Social Movements* (Amherst: University of Massachusetts Press, 2000), p. 16.

2. Howard Zinn, *The Politics of History* (Chicago: University of Illinois Press, 1990), p. 47.

3. Edward Chambers, *Roots for Radicals: Organizing for Power, Action and Justice* (New York: Continuum, 2003), p. 22.

4. James Green, *Taking History to Heart: The Power of the Past in Building Social Movements* (Amherst: University of Massachusetts Press, 2000), p. 11.

Chapter 8

1. Jo Ann Gibson Robinson, *The Montgomery Bus Boycott and the Women Who Started It: The Memoir of Jo Ann Gibson Robinson* (Knoxville: University of Tennessee Press, 1987), p. viii.

2. Ibid., p. 45.

3. Ibid., pp. 45–46.

4. Paula Giddings, *When and Where I Enter: The Impact of Black Women on Race and Sex in America* (New York: Bantam Books, 1984), p. 266.

5. Martin Luther King Jr., *Stride toward Freedom: The Montgomery Story* (New York: Harper & Row, 1958), p. ix.

6. Jim Collins, *Good to Great: Why Some Companies Make the Leap—and Others Don't* (New York: HarperBusiness, 2001), pp. 164–65.

7. Paul Rogat Loeb, *Soul of a Citizen: Living with Conviction in a Cynical Time* (New York: St. Martin's Press, 1999), p. 41.

8. Ibid., p. 260.

9. Philip Dray, *At Hands of Persons Unknown: The Lynching of Black America* (New York: Random House, 2002), pp. 360, 361.

10. Ibid., p. 432.

Chapter 9

1. Freire, *Pedagogy of the Oppressed,* p. 42.

2. Rogat Loeb, *Soul of a Citizen,* p. 54.

3. Gibson Robinson, *Montgomery Bus Boycott,* p. 60.

Acknowledgments

New York City is a massive metropolis, but in the organizing and housing worlds it can feel more like a small town—a handful of rabble-rousers getting together every few weeks to take on the next target. I was lucky to know the following organizing friends and allies, many of whom helped contribute to this book in formal and informal ways: Jennifer Flynn at the New York City AIDS Housing Network; Sam J. Miller at Picture the Homeless; Andrew Friedman at Make the Road by Walking; Artemio Guerra at the Fifth Avenue Committee (*y La Unión de la Comunidad Latina*); and Dave Powell, longtime radical punk (and voted "best housing activist" by the *Village Voice*).

Veteran organizer Alfredo deAvila at the Applied Research Center—formerly with the Center for Third World Organizing—was a critical source of information and inspiration. He swooped in from Oakland several times a year full of manic energy. Within an hour he'd be scribbling out ingenious campaigns on scraps of paper, all the while shouting "Just do it, *chavo!*" or "Cut it out!"

whenever he didn't agree with something I was saying. Our lead paint campaign, in particular, wouldn't have occurred without Alfredo's guidance.

PACC was a great place to work, and to meet incredible people. Along with hundreds of members—too numerous to name here—I'd like to especially thank Steve Aronson, Deb Howard, Amy Laura Cahn, Enida Davis, Jedidah Baptiste, Anne Lessy, Elizabeth Mendoza, Annie Mae Dawson, Yeneika Puran, Julieta Padilla, America Rivera, Hector Rivera, *Señor* Enrique, *La Jefa* Juanita, Margarita Rivera, Jackie E. Mitchell, Pastor John Graepel, Alan Rivera, Adriana Mendoza, and Reverend David Dyson.

After the drudgery of high school, I was fortunate to have the chance to hang out with three stellar professors at the University of Redlands: David Tharp, James Sandos, and Jennifer Keene (now at Chapman University). Their passion for history and ideas (not to mention radical politics) influenced the direction of my life, and this book. At college I also made friends—a motley group of alienated geniuses—who at various times listened to me ramble on about organizing. Thanks especially to Pat Heninger, Nathan Tenney, Diami Virgilio, Lynsee Sardell, Lauren Cooper, and Javanica Curry.

I will always be grateful to Michael Bourret of Dystel & Goderich Literary Management for signing on with an unknown author. The publishing world can be a brutal and depressing place, but not if you're lucky enough to have the right guide. Thanks also to Carl Bromley at Nation Books for providing helpful feedback and a genuine enthusiasm for ideas, and to Anne Sullivan, who does the exhausting behind the scenes work of book publicity with wild enthusiasm and amazing efficiency. Speaking of amazing efficiency, serious praise is due to Web guru Amanda Luker for designing this book's Web site (as well as my own homepage). Check out her other fabulous work at www.pinkslipmedia.org.

The same hometown crowd that supported my first book was steadfastly behind me again. If you're reading this, it's quite possibly because my parents shoved it in your face and demanded you purchase it. You made the right decision: they're very determined. From our first exploratory telephone conversations years ago, my parents, Jim Thompson and Sandra Hietala, never seemed to doubt that this book would be published. Their optimism, in turn, is due in part to their wonderful parents, Marjorie Bjerkager and Ralph and Ivy Hietala (along with my late grandfathers Bill Thompson and Orville Bjerkager—both radicals in their own ways).

Organizing for social change is an endurance activity. At PACC, I followed in the footsteps of a determined, compassionate, feisty, dedicated, combative, and unabashedly *radical* organizer named Daniella Ponet. We've been together for five years now. Daniella helped me think through many of the ideas in the book and read numerous early drafts with her sharp eye and unrivaled editing prowess. I look forward to watching her radical vision unfold in the coming years.

Index